COMMUNICATING IN CHINESE

an interactive approach to beginning Chinese

Teacher's Activity Book for Listening and Speaking

Cynthia Ning

University of Hawai'i

Far Eastern Publications
Yale University

Copyright @ 1993, by Far Eastern Publications
Yale University

Library of Congress Cataloging in Publications Data:

Ning, Cynthia
    COMMUNICATING IN CHINESE: Teacher's Activity Book 1

    1. Chinese language-Grammar
    2. Chinese language-Textbooks for foreign speakers-
       English
    3. Teacher's Manual

    ISBN 0-88710-176-3

    Printed in the United States of America

    10 9 8 7 6 5 4 3 2 1

.......................CONTENTS

COMMUNICATING
IN CHINESE

INTRODUCTION

The focus on proficiency treats foreign language learning as a SKILLS-based program, with the entry point being not grammar but the functional use of language. A proficiency-based program is built upon a sequence of functions in context, from the most fundamental (introducing yourself in an informal, social context, for example) to the more complex (expressing disagreement in a formal, business context, for example). Grammar is subsumed to function and context: only those structures that are necessary to carry out a particular task in a particular context are utilized. Thus where the grammar-based curriculum might introduce three uses of the particle le quite early, the proficiency (function/context)-based curriculum might not focus on any particular use of le until it became necessary for a student to express him/herself using a function of le—say in a lesson on how to refuse further assistance (Chi bao le, xiexie; buyao le, xiexie).

Conversely, any structure that is necessary to carry out a particular task would be introduced, regardless of its "complexity" and its position in the hierarchy of the grammar-based curriculum. In an early lesson on meeting and getting to know people, for instance, the sentence Qing ba ni de dizhi xiexialai might be introduced, not as the ba construction per se, but simply as a lexical unit to be learned for this particular context.

Thus, a proficiency-based program is one in which goals and objectives are set in terms of performance standards, which includes but is not defined in terms of grammatical accuracy.

If students are to be trained to function in the target culture, they need to begin to practise to function in the target language, in the classroom, as soon and as much as possible, with as great a degree of linguistic and cultural accuracy as possible, and in as many contexts as possible.

The most valuable resource available to teacher and students in the classroom, that is not available anywhere else, is themselves—their collective experience, knowledge, talent, interests, and single purpose—to learn the foreign language. The congregation of students and instructor(s) in class affords an opportunity for person-to-person interaction, that will not be duplicated elsewhere. No text, tape, or other mechanically recorded program can approximate the range, resourcefulness, and responsiveness of the human mind (although computer programs can extend and supplement particular functions). Readings, writing practice, tape exercises, grammar explanations, computer exploration exercises and the like may be useful but can be profitably accomplished elsewhere, outside of class.

In class, the teacher's most important role is to facilitate purposeful interaction among the students, using the target language. Such interaction is most profitable to the learner when it involves activities that are a) communicative—in which real (not merely simulated) communication takes place, b) task-based—that is, centered on the successful completion of a task (which is not simply accurate language production), and c) interactive—involving the negotiation of meaning between two or more participants.

Real life communication is purposeful. We communicate in order to obtain or give information to achieve an end (purchase a ticket, make an appointment), even if the end is simply to establish or maintain useful social ties ("catching up" with an old acquaintance). Learning language via communicative, task-based activities means gaining practice in dealing with real life, except that through the mediation of the teacher, "life-like" tasks are made more manageable for the student, and the information to be learned is therefore presented in more manageable increments.

If the activity is *communicative*, there is an exchange of real, relevant information between participants. A conversation such as the following: "Am I the teacher?" "Yes you are the teacher." "Are you the student?" "Yes I am the student." does not, under normal circumstances, impart any real information. The focus of this activity (the conversation) is not communicative.

Take another hypothetical conversation. "What do you like to do?" "I like to swim." "What does your mother like to do?" "She likes to mow the lawn." "What does your father like to do?" "He likes to go shopping." "What does your uncle like to do?" etc. While such a conversation might convey real information, it doesn't readily appear relevant. Real communication is an exchange of information that pertains to a task or an issue at hand. The person asking questions in the conversation described does not appear purposeful; the activity is, on the face of it, not task-based. When an activity is *task-based*, students have to achieve an end which is not simply to produce language. By this definition, legitimate tasks include the following: "Find out where the department store is (in a hypothetical city)," or "Find out who in this class is wearing the most expensive shoes," or "Line up your five blocks (each of which is a different color) in the same order as my five blocks (which you cannot see)." On the other hand, "Ask five "where" questions" or "Make a statement using past tense" are not legitimate tasks, since the goal of these is no more than the accurate production of language.

Finally, an *interactive* activity allows for the negotiation of meaning. It encourages each participant to assume reasonable control of its progress, to begin and to encourage communication, to confirm and correct understanding, to expand upon or to redirect current communication, to determine when the interaction should end, and to bring the interaction to a close. Students should learn and practice to pose their own questions as necessary, press for repetition or clarification, respond when queried, and decide when they have enough information for their purposes and may end the exchange. Since traditionally classes are teacher-controlled, the focus on interactivity means that students are allowed, or coerced, to actively devise means to obtain and provide necessary information—and not merely to interpret information when it happens to be provided by the teacher or the text.

Literature on foreign language education has stressed that proficiency is not a method but an orientation. It is not the Silent Way, Total Physical Response, Suggestopedia, the Natural Approach, but it can include as much as is useful from any of those methodologies and more, in order to best achieve the goals and objectives set for the program. Grammar-translation and Audiolingualism have been superceded, but teachers have on occasion used techniques from those methodologies to some benefit in the classroom. Regardless of what methodologies the teacher chooses to use, the following principles should be considered.

1.   Principles in implementing the curriculum

The ideal environment for the high-school or college learner of foreign languages would combine the advantages of the childhood environment—in which the first language was acquired—with the cognitive resources available to the mature learner. In early childhood the language learner is uninhibited and highly motivated, and lives in an environment rich in language input. The mature learner on the other hand has greater cognitive ability and experiential knowledge than the child, and is better able to structure learning for maximum gain. We can posit, then, that the teacher's task is to assist in creating a class environment that includes some of the advantages of the childhood setting, but that facilitates a richer and more focused flow of information to suit the capacity of the older learner.

Following are some principles in curriculum implementation, to maximize benefit to the learner.

1.1 Disinhibition

Children typically have high motivation and a low anxiety level in acquiring new language. In this regard, cultivating a goal-directed sense of *playfulness* in the classroom would be helpful. Students should be encouraged to be *serious* in regard to the *objectives* but *playful* vis-a-vis the *process* of learning a foreign language. The process of learning to communicate in a foreign language must include tentative probes and tumbles, risk-taking, trial and error. A beginning foreign language learner is necessarily insecure about his or her communicative capabilities. A playful classroom atmosphere can help to reduce anxiety and increase tolerance for insecurity, and thus enhance language learning. On the other hand, seriousness vis-a-vis language learning objectives—including working to become systematically more secure session by session—ensures that playfulness does not get so out of hand that it detracts from language learning.

1.2 Empowerment

Here this term means building student involvement and self-confidence by sharing some of a teacher's "power" with them.

First and foremost, knowledge is power. That the teacher possesses the knowledge base relevant to the class is taken for granted; the challenge is to keep the students from feeling that they have no relevant knowledge to bring to class. As much as possible, activities should make use of students' previous knowledge of given topics, some of which may be new to the teacher. Brainstorming activities, for example, allow the teacher to learn the point of departure in a new lesson, and the students to have some hand in creating the content of a lesson. Such an activity contrasts with lessons based entirely on teacher-selected texts, in which the teacher alone asks questions to which she has all the answers. Empowering students may increase the challenge for teachers. Often the teacher will be asked to deal with unfamiliar items, even if she is a native speaker of the target language. It may in fact be helpful for the student to see the teacher taking risks, making mistakes, and admitting "I don't know (but I will find out)" on occasion.

Expressing one's own meaning in the foreign language is power. Students struggling to express their own ideas will, upon succeeding, have gained more useful knowledge than those instructed to translate the teacher's (or the textbook author's) ideas into Chinese. If nothing else, they will learn to control their own expectations of what they can reasonably hope to express in the foreign language—a useful skill by any measure.

Requesting that students assist in preparing classroom activities is not only another form of empowerment, it may be a neccessity for the overworked language instructor. Students often have more creativity, talent, and drive than an individual teacher may be able to muster. A bank of test items for instance may be created by the students, then selected or modified by the teacher to include on quizzes and exams.

Finally, the right to evaluate others also constitutes classroom power. Occasional grading by peers can serve multiple purposes of empowering those peers, exposing the student being evaluated to critique from a source other than the teacher, and giving the students an understanding of what the teacher must take into consideration in assigning scores.

1.3 Focus on learning

It is not sufficient for a teacher to say, "I covered this topic in class, so the students should know it." One cannot assume that simply because a particular skill has been "taught," it has necessarily been "learned." The teacher is only justified in asserting that the skill has been learned when the students can demonstrate (through competent performance in a simulated or real-life context) that they indeed have gained creative control over that skill. For instance, discussion and a round of practice in making telephone appointments in class may not have been enough to ensure that the students actually know how to make such appointments; a performance check (say by having students pretend to call each other in class, or actually call you or another native speaker outside of class) will reveal how much the student has actually learned. Progress can only be measured by how much has been *learned*, not by how much has been *taught*.

1.4 Receptive before productive skills

Most of the introduction and drilling activities suggested in this manual allow the students to listen purposefully to language samples and to demonstrate comprehension in a way that does not require oral production of the new material. Similarly, it is suggested that reading (as a receptive skill) precede writing (a productive skill); that a particular reading unit be taught with sufficient lead time to allow it to blend into the corpus of "familiar material", before introducing writing and writing tasks based on the same unit. The basis of this tenet is that as students are engaged in purposeful listening and reading activities, they are forming essential hypotheses about the language that they begin to test once they embark on productive skills. Forcing production on students before they have adequate information about language forms through receptive exercises can hamper production.

1.5 Student as resource

In the classroom, students are not only the target of instruction, they are the greatest resource available to the teacher as well. Their physical characteristics, personalities, opinions, talents, experiences, and even their imaginations and creativity can be the most productive audio-visual aid available to assist with instruction.

The sequences "Hideko has short hair, Mary has long hair, Epi has very long hair," or "Tom is wearing a blue shirt, Muhammed is wearing a white shirt, Junhua is wearing a green shirt" are easy examples of student-centered instruction (the names representing real students), where the task at hand is the introduction of vocabulary in a lesson on personal description. More abstract concepts can be pantomimed nicely by students, while the teacher models the language (see Pantomime below).

At intervals, student compositions (after correction and revision) can become listening or reading materials for the class. Brief compositions along the lines of "I am 5'6" and 120 lbs. I am a college freshman. I have black eyes and brown hair. I like to wear a purple sweatshirt. Who am I?" can either be read aloud to the class or photocopied and passed out as a reading exercise for the class, which then guesses the identities of the authors.

1.6 Uneven mastery of material

This has to do with the notions of *conceptual, partial,* and *full* control of information. Under conceptual control, the student has been introduced to new information, forms an understanding of its uses, and is about to begin internalizing it. At this stage she is not familiar enough with the information to make use of it. With partial control, she has gained enough familiarity with the material to begin to use it, although inappropriately or erroneously at times. After an extended period of ever improving but still partial control, the student eventually gains full control, at which point she can use the material freely and effectively.

For the learner of the native language, the transition from conceptual to full control of material is a continuum. New information is constantly available. Full control of bits of new information is sometimes quickly obtained, but most of it can only be learned over an extended period of time, after repeated contact in different contexts. There is some information over which even the educated native speaker will never gain full control, since partial control suffices. Technical vocabulary and jargon, for instance, may be vaguely familiar to most educated native speakers, who will not likely have enough control of it to use it productively.

The implication for the classroom is this: too often textbooks and teachers who teach the textbook prepare a limited curriculum for the students, with the expectation that everything covered is to be mastered by the end of the course. By this reasoning, since the amount of material over which students can reasonably be expected to have full control is limited, the materials for the course must therefore be strictly limited as well. Thus the student, if he does well, gains a certain amount of confidence in severely limited patches (which is the extent of the curriculum) of a very large universe (which is the target language), without being exposed to the depth and breadth of that universe, and without obtaining the wherewithal to continue to navigate and to learn in that universe, once he leaves the confines of his language classroom. Course objectives that focus on conceptual and partial control over a larger spectrum of material serve to expose the students to more of the universe of the foreign language than those that target full control alone. A student with conceptual or partial control of a wide range of topics, and full control over some, is arguably better equipped to handle the foreign universe than one who has full mastery over a severely limited range.

1.7   Toleration of uncertainty

This principle concerns classroom simulation of real life foreign language contexts. In the target culture, the student would be confronted with situations in which a large part of what she hears and sees is unfamiliar. It is thus in the student's best interests to develop a tolerance for uncertainty, to learn to maintain composure in the face of incomprehensible input. With training, students can learn to extract meaning by using all language skills at her disposal, to guess from context and known information, to make use of non-verbal indicators, to listen selectively, to skim and scan written texts, etc.

The classroom teacher can begin by incorporating measured doses of unfamiliar material, including material to be covered in future lessons, or even material that will never appear anywhere in the curriculum, over parts of which the student can eventually be expected to develop some conceptual or even partial control, as a result of repeated exposure. Incorporating this principle into classroom teaching also gives teachers far greater freedom to use carefully calibrated but authentic language: in her own daily classroom instructions to the students, in dialogues between native speakers, in radio and television broadcasts, in reading materials selected from authentic texts, etc., all of which will include much that is unfamiliar to the students.

1.8   Uneven progression in the four skills

A child acquiring a language naturally is likely to come into contact with new vocabulary and structures first aurally—i.e. by listening, comprehending, and perhaps learning—then at a later date using the new material in speech, then even later encountering the material in writing and thus learning to read and comprehend it, and finally finding the need in some different context to produce the new material in writing. It is highly unlikely that all four skills would be learned as a single unit. Parents simply would not say to a child, "BATHTUB, Johnny, BATHTUB. Listen, BATHTUB. Now say it, BATHTUB. Now read it, B-A-T-H-T-U-B. Now write it, and <u>after</u> you demonstrate to my satisfaction that you can write BATHTUB correctly, I will teach you FAUCET." This is not to say that, with adult learners, one can not work purposefully on developing reading skills in order to stretch speaking skills or vice versa; simply that the four skills need not necessarily be taught as one indivisible unit, as was previously the case, particularly in Chinese language programs.

Mastery of all four skills should by no means be required for all material. It is widely known that native speakers of a language have different vocabularies in listening, speaking, reading, and writing; why should we attempt to impose uniformity on our students? Flexibility in four-skills coverage of a topic is particularly important in a language such as Chinese, in which general speech is colloquial, but writing is mostly classical. That is, not all material covered in a spoken curriculum need be reduplicated in written form, and conversely, not all material read or written need be learned in speech.

2. Suggested classroom activities

Classroom time should as much as possible be spent interactively, communicatively. While it might be necessary to occasionally respond (briefly!) to a question regarding vocabulary or grammar, the majority of class time should be devoted to activities such as the following (given in alphabetical order).

2.1 Brainstorming

After the sentence pattern(s) and new vocabulary for a lesson have been introduced in one or more introduction and drill sessions, take approximately 10 minutes and have the students create phrases, statements, and questions based on the content of the new lesson, perhaps combined with what they remember of previous lessons. Encourage them to create with the language (within reasonable bounds), to guess at how meaning might be rendered in Chinese, based on what they know. Record what they say (corrected as necessary) on an overhead transparency. After the period is over, photocopy (or retype and then photocopy) your record and distribute to the students. They may study and review it as they do the language samples in the textbook.

2.2 Card drills

Separate packs of playing cards into individual suites (hearts, clubs, spades, diamonds). Remove the Jacks, Kings, Queens, and Jokers; tell the students that the Aces represent the number "1," and the 10s represent the number "0." Have the students form pairs, and distribute one suite to each pair. Have students take turns drilling their partners on numbers by laying down one card at a time and having the partner identify the number or the amount thus created, up to, five or six cards in a row. Each new card goes to the RIGHT of the person stating the numbers. The first card put down cannot be the card 10 representing the number "0". One drill session might proceed as follows.

(Tutor)   (Tutee)

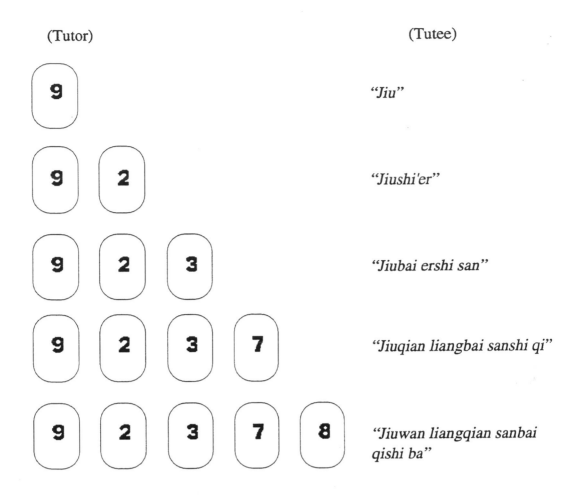

9					"Jiu"
9	**2**				"Jiushi'er"
9	**2**	**3**			"Jiubai ershi san"
9	**2**	**3**	**7**		"Jiuqian liangbai sanshi qi"
9	**2**	**3**	**7**	**8**	"Jiuwan liangqian sanbai qishi ba"

If the content to be drilled was money, each successive card would indicate increasing amounts. Following the sample above, the tutee's responses would begin with "<u>Jiu fen qian</u>," and proceed to "<u>Jiu mao liang fen qian</u>," "<u>Jiu kuai liang mao san fen qian</u>," etc.

Card drills should be repeated throughout the early years of language instruction, since numbers are basic to survival language, and students seldom become familiar with them in the one or two sessions that are typically devoted to number study in a foreign language curriculum.

2.3 Class roster

Type the names of all students in the class in a single column. Underline the spaces next to each name, to create a line on which information about each student can be written. This is the class roster. Photocopy it so that each student receives one. Ask the students to Mingle (see below), and collect specific information from each person named on the roster, depending on the content of the lesson: telephone number, birthday, favorite color, etc., and to record that information in the space provided next to the person's name. If the information to be collected is simple and each exchange is therefore short, the students can try to "interview" everyone in the class. Otherwise, the activity can end after a specified period of time (say, 10-15 minutes). Before the activity begins, model two or three interchanges with student volunteers, so that you are sure the students know what is expected of them. After the activity is over, check the accuracy of the information gathered as a group. Review several ways of asking and answering the questions the students had to pose, to obtain the information sought.

2.4 Communication-gap activities

Many examples of these are contained in the materials provided for each lesson in this Teacher's Guide. Others can be obtained from books such as <u>Elementary Communication Games</u> by Jill Hadfield (Nelson, 1984). These activities are set up so that each participant possesses a portion of the information necessary to carry out an objective, and must communicate with each other to obtain all of the information necessary. When you become familiar with common techniques used to devise such activities, you may wish to construct some of your own, to fit your particular needs. They commonly require advanced preparation: statement of the task, instructions to the students, and some props (generally pictures, lists, written descriptions).

It is important to keep in mind that the students need to be properly prepared to carry out the activity. Communication-gap activities are usually not effective as introduction or drills for new materials, but as an opportunity to apply skills already learned (controlled use of materials). Before beginning the activity, the teacher should lead the class in brainstorming the language necessary to carry out the task assigned in the activity, and should ensure that the students fully understand the procedure involved, perhaps by demonstrating it with one or more volunteers.

2.5 Divergent activities

Most classroom activities described in this *Guide* are *convergent*, that is, they focus on a limited set of structures or vocabulary, and are intended to afford practice within that delineated set. Divergent activities on the other hand plumb the depths of the students brains, so to speak, to see what lies dormant there. These activities are good to do every so often, to help consolidate the pieces of information the students have been learning, either as a scheduled part of the curriculum, or as a "filler" whenever five to fifteen minutes remain in the period after all planned activities have been carried out. Following are some examples of divergent activities.

2.5.1 Asking questions

Divide the class into groups of 3-5. Give each group about 20 index cards, and ask them, as a group, to make up 15-20 questions. They should write these questions down, one per card. Set a time limit, say 10 minutes, for them to complete the assignment. When they are done, draw lots or otherwise assign an order in which the groups are going to have a chance to ask their questions. Give each group a number based on this order. Then proceed as follows with the question game.

Make a grid on the blackboard, with space to record the points that each group accumulates.

Have the members of group 1 begin to take turns asking 10 of their questions, one question at a time. The other groups compete to answer these questions. (As soon as one member of an "answering" group know the answer to a question posed by the "questioning" group, she raises her hand. The first person to raise a hand gets a chance to answer a question. You may wish to make it a rule that no one in any group can get to "go again" until everyone in the group has "gone" once; of course, they may coach each other.)

A correct question wins a point.

A correct question that contains vocabulary or structures incomprehensible to the others must be explained (in Chinese) by the group posing it. If the "answering" groups subsequently understand the question well enough so that someone can answer it, the "questioning" group wins a point for that question.

The maximum number of points a group can win for asking questions is 10.

Once a question has been asked, no other group can ask precisely the same question. They will have to dig among their "spare" questions for a replacement.

Every correct answer wins a point.

Once group 1 has either won 10 points or asked all the questions they made up, the turn rotates to group 2. Proceed through all the groups.

The group with the highest score wins.

2.5.2 Description

Place an item on the table (a figurine, a cultural object, a daily use object), or show a picture or a slide, and have the students make statements or ask and answer questions about it. Write all their utterances down on an overhead transparency. Make copies of the transparency, hand out one per student, and have them write a descriptive paragraph of the item in pinyin, characters, or a combination of the two, for homework. As an alternative for something to describe, bring in a picture, poster, cartoon, slide—anything that is interesting and relevant to what you are doing.

2.5.3 Free association

Write a word, a phrase, a sentence, or a sentence pattern on the blackboard, to serve as the "tag." Invite the students to say anything they can in the target language, incorporating the "tag" into their sentence. Supposing you write mai dongxi. The students might say the following:

> *Wo xihuan mai dongxi.*
> *Wo yao mai dongxi, keshi meiyou qian.*
> *Wo changchang mai dongxi.*
> *Ni yao qu mai dongxi ma?*
> *Shei qu mai dongxi le?*
> *Women shenme shihou qu mai dongxi?* etc.

To give them an incentive to make up as many sentences as possible, you might turn the activity into a game. Divide the class into two teams. List the members of each team on the board, in two columns. Invite everyone to raise their hand when they have a statement or question in mind. Alternate from team to team when you call on students. If the student makes an utterance that is correct, check off his name on the board. If the utterance is comprehensible but not correct, first correct it, and then have the student restate it. Then check off his name on the board. If the utterance is incomprehensible, say "Duibuqi, wo budong," and give someone else on the same team a chance. Note however, that no-one may speak a second time in the same round, until all members of his team have spoken once. Thus if the student whose utterance is incomprehensible is the only one on the team who hasn't yet spoken, he will lose the round for the team. Unobtrusive coaching by team-mates is allowable; duplicate utterances are not.

A team wins a point when the rival team is no longer able to come up with an allowable utterance.

After a point is awarded, select a new tag, erase all check-marks from the board, and begin the next round. The game is over when one team makes a predetermined number of points (3? 4?), or when a prespecified period of time has passed (10-15 minutes).

2.5.4 Interview

Invite a native speaker (or any fluent speaker) of Chinese to class. Do not introduce her to the students; allow them to ask questions freely, try to comprehend the responses, and take notes (in English) about specifics of what the interviewee says. After a specified period of time (say 10 minutes), have the students form groups to pool their information, and, based on this information, to make up questions to pose to the other groups in the class. Ideally, the interviewee should remain in the room to check on the accuracy of the responses. Award points as follows.

Each comprehensible and acceptable question earns a point for the group that poses it.

Anyone in the responding groups may volunteer to answer; call on the first one to raise a hand, and allow 3 seconds for the response. If it is correct, award that group a point. No-one in the group should respond a second time until everyone in the group has responded once; coaching is allowed.

If the response is wrong, the turn passes to another group (first one to signal gets the turn).

If no responding group can answer correctly, the group that posed the question may do so. If their response is correct, they receive a second point. If not, they LOSE 2 points.

2.5.5 Role-play

Form the students into pairs or small groups. Give each a role-play card (examples are given in Appendix 1 of this volume), and have them carry out the task assigned. You may wish to give each pair or small group a tape recorder, ask them to practice their assignment a while, and then make a recording of their best work. (They may wish to check with you each time they are ready to record an utterance, to make sure it is accurate.) Have the groups swap tapes and critique them.

2.5.6 Twenty questions

Played just as the parlor game, this activity presents the students an opportunity to formulate and pose a wide range of questions. "It" thinks of an item (say, "kuaizi," and the class attempts to guess what it is. The other participants would have to ask yes/no questions to narrow down by category the range that fits the item; "Shi ren ma? Shi difang ma? Shi dongxi ma?" etc. To provide a model of the kinds of questions possible, the teacher should allow the whole class to be "it" for a round or two, and ask all the questions. Then the teacher can be "it" and the class guesses, and finally the teacher can become simply an advisor, and a student or a pair of students can take over the role of "it."

It is possible to pre-set the scope of the activity by determining a context, say shopping for clothes or dinner at a restaurant, to fit the content of current instruction.

2.6 Games

Competition is motivating, provided that the spirit of competition is not taken so far as to create undue stress. Games usually require team-work, and therefore can serve to prod the non-participatory student into participation. Most importantly, students tend to enjoy them. The challenge for the teacher is create games that maximize effective language use by the students—in which most class time is spent "on task." Examples of common games:

2.6.1 "The Big Wind Blows" (Da feng chui)

This is a variation on "Musical Chairs." Students draw their chairs into a large circle, arranging them to allow easy access to each chair. The teacher stands in the middle of the circle, and begins a "chant." The original "chant" of the Chinese game is as follows:

Teacher:	*Da feng chui.*	(The big wind blows.)
Students (in chorus):	*Chui shenme?*	(At what does it blow?)
Teacher:	*Chui....chang toufa de ren!*	
	(It blows at....people with long hair!)	

At this point, all students with long hair must quickly get up and exchange seats. In the melee, the teacher secures a seat and sits down, leaving one student stranded in the center of the circle to continue the "chant." When this student gets to the ending (underlined portion), she substitutes a phrase of her creation (nanhaizi, chuan qunzi de ren, xue Zhongwen de ren, etc.). The game continues for a predetermined period of time. The original chant might be modified to make it more pedagogically redeeming (based on more usable phrases), perhaps as follows:

Teacher:	*Wo zai zhao ren.*	(I am looking for someone/some people.)
Students:	*Ni zhao shei?*	(Who are you looking for?)
Teacher:	*Wo zhao..chang toufa de ren!*	
	(I'm looking for....people with long hair!)	

To fit the game to the content of a specific lesson, you may wish to hand out a card with a vocabulary item on it to each student, and then fit the "chant" to that vocabulary. Say that at the beginning of the year you are working on numbers. If each student has a random number, then the "chant" might include "Wo zai zhao shuzi!" "Ni zhao shenme shuzi?" "Wo zhao 1 dao 8!" or "Wo zhao shuang hao!" If the lesson focuses on countries, each student would role-play one nationality, and the "chant" might include "Wo zhao Ouzhou ren!" or "Wo zhao Zhongguo ren, Riben ren, gen Hanguo ren!"

2.6.2 Charades

This is useful to review the contents of specific lessons. Write out 5-6 sentences (in *pinyin*) based on what you wish to review (say, the unit on food: "Wo xiang he yidian dongxi" "Wo bu xihuan chi doufu" etc.). Divide your class into teams of 4-7 students each. Have each team send up a representative, show the representatives one sentence, make sure each understands and remembers the sentence (whisper!), and then on a signal, go back to his or her team and act out the sentence (in standard "Charades" format). The first team to get the sentence exactly right wins a point. Proceed till all points have been awarded.

2.6.3 Hungry Ghosts

In some popular games the class stands in a circle, performs a succession of tasks, and each student who gets a task wrong "drops out" of the game (see "Simon Says" below). The problem with having more and more students "out" of the game is that eventually most of the students are no longer engaged in the activity. In Hungry Ghosts format, the failed student does not drop out for good. He simply becomes a Hungry Ghost (the uneasy spirits of Chinese tradition that prey on the living), selects one of his classmates who is still in the game, and hovers menacingly behind this classmate. When the classmate goofs, the Ghost displaces him and returns to the game (and the "living"), while the new Ghost goes on to haunt someone else. The game proceeds for a set period of time.

2.6.4 Simon Says

This is an old children's game in which one player gives all the other players a sequence of instructions, of which only those instructions preceded by "Simon Says" are to be followed. A player who carries out an instruction ("Touch your nose!") that is not preceded by "Simon Says" ("Simon says, touch your nose!") is out of the game, as is a player who does not carry out an instruction that is preceded by "Simon Says." For classroom purposes, it would be better to substitute a useful phrase (such as *"Qing...," "Mafan ni..."*) for "Simon Says." Also, the unsuccessful student should become a Hungry Ghost (see above) rather than drop out of the game.

2.7 Group work

Sometimes it is useful to put students in groups of up to five students (more than that becomes cumbersome) and have them work on a task together. (Several are described in this manual; see Unit 5c: Rummage Sale.) Working in a group allows students to develop turn-taking strategies.

2.8 Guessing

This is a convenient way of introducing new material, that makes use of any previous knowledge the students may have. Say the content of the new lesson is color terms. Hold up two color cards—blue and red for instance—say "Zheige shi hongde," and have the students point to the one they think you refer to. At least half of the class is likely to pick the right color. Hold up the red card to confirm that those who picked red were right, then put that card down and pick up, say, the green one. Say "Zheige shi lüde" and repeat the process. If any of the students have even the vaguest recollection of having heard the word for "green" before, they will likely point to the right card, however hesitantly. In any case, each student has a 50% chance of being right. Continue through all the new items, and repeat the cycle two or three times. With each successive repetition the students' ability to identify the correct card increases, and their willingness to take a chance and make an educated guess at meaning in the target language also increases.

2.9 High-low

If the content of the lesson involves numbers (street numbers, height, weight, prices, dates, times, sizes of clothing, temperature, distance, population, etc.), *High-low* can be used as a drill for both receptive and productive skills. Supposing the lesson involves prices. The teacher begins by arbitrarily selecting a price (without revealing it to the class), writing it in large numbers on a piece of paper taped face down to the blackboard or on a spot on the black-board that is covered by a piece of paper, having the class guess what price was selected, and the teacher responding "higher" or "lower" to the guesses. For instance, if the teacher selected the price $74.98, the exchange might go as follows.

Student 1: *Wushi kuai qian.*	Teacher: *Gui yidiar.*
Student 2: *Yibai kuai qian.*	Teacher: *Pianyi yidiar.*
Student 3: *Liushi kuai qian.*	Teacher: *Gui yidiar.*

And so on until the exact price is guessed. It would help to write each guess on the black-board as the student makes it, replacing previous guesses, to provide the current range between which subsequent guesses should continue. In later rounds, a student may take over the teacher's role (with the teacher as advisor).

To drill times and dates, the teacher's responses might be "zao yidiar/wan yidiar," for distance "yuan yidiar/jin yidiar," for height "gao yidiar/ai yidiar," for temperature "re yidiar/leng yidiar," for size of clothing "da yidiar/xiao yidiar," for population "duo yidiar/ shao yidiar," etc.

2.10 Inner-outer circles

For a class that tends to become rowdy or misdirected, this is an effective way to have students interact briefly with a large number of their classmates. (Other ways to achieve such interaction include *Mingling* and *Visiting* (see below)). Divide the class into two groups. One group forms a circle, facing outwards. When the circle is formed, the other group matches up one-on-one to the first group, thus forming a second circle that faces inwards. The pairs created in this fashion interact briefly (a minute or two), and upon a signal from the teacher, the outer circle rotates one person to the right. Continue as necessary. If there are an uneven number of students in the class, either participate in the activity yourself, or have two students double up as a "permanent pair," and interact with a third student.

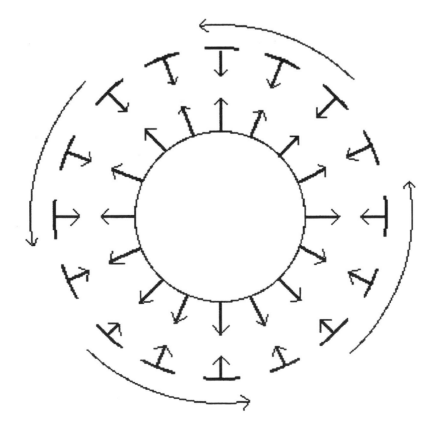

2.11   Line-up

When lesson content includes a numerical concept (height, time, distance) or some very clear form of gradation (colors in a spectrum), this is a convenient and very effective way to have students practice asking and answering relevant questions. The activity is simple. Say the lesson is on birthdays. Have the students line up by order of their birthdays, from the earliest in the year on one end of the line, to the latest in the year on the other. In order to find out where in line they belong, each student will have to ask "<u>Ni de shengri shi jiyue jihao</u>?" of many of their classmates. After the line-up is complete, go down the line (or around the circle, if your classroom is small) and have the students call out their answers, to check that each student's position in line is correct. Other suitable topics include telephone numbers (lowest number to highest number), height, distance from home to school, etc. You may choose to assign an attribute to the students (give him/her a slip of paper with a date and time for an appointment), and have them line up according to that.

2.12   Mingling

Students pretend they are at a cocktail party, stand up, and move from class-mate to class-mate sociably and at their own speed. Of course, they will be trying to complete a communicative assignment you have given them as they "mingle." The teacher may either mingle with the students and attempt to carry out the task as well, thereby interacting with the students and checking out their performance, or may simply wander around, eavesdrop, and answer questions as they arise. The activity can end either when the teacher senses that students have completed the task, or when a predetermined period of time has elapsed.

2.13   Pair-work

The simplest form of pair-work is when the teacher instructs, "Turn to your neighbor and greet them," or "Turn to your neighbor and find out their telephone number," based on what you happen to be working on in the lesson. To provide more practice, this can be followed up with "Now turn to your OTHER neighbor and (repeat the same task)" or "Now turn to the person behind or in front of you and (repeat the same task)." For communication-gap activities that require pairs, you may wish to consciously put together certain pairs so that one may tutor the other, or conversely randomly assign pairs so that students interact with someone other than a neighbor. There are many ways to assign random pairs. One simple way is to start at any point in the room and have the students count off, up to a number that equals half the students in the class. The following student begins again at one and the rest of the students count off in order to the number equalling half the number of students in the class again. "Ones" work together as a pair, as do "twos," "threes," "fours," etc. If there is an odd student out, that student either works with one of the pairs as a triplet, or pairs up with the teacher.

Another way is to hand out prepared matched slips, one to a student, and ask them to mingle until they find their match. One of a set of matched slips might have a Chinese term (<u>xuexiao</u>) on it and the other its English definition ("school"); or one of the slips might have a Chinese character and the other its *pinyin* rendition. A more challenging technique involves stimulus-response or cause-consequence; one slip may say "<u>Wo e le</u>" and the other "<u>Wo qu chi dongxi</u>," or one may say "<u>Zheige dongxi tai guile</u>" and the other "<u>Wo bu mai</u>," for instance.

2.14   Pantomime

This is a fun and simple way to introduce new material that is as popular with high school as with adult learners. Supposing you are working with a lesson on professions. Ask for a volunteer pantomimist to come to the front of the class. Point to the English definition of a word you want her to pantomime (say, <u>jingcha</u>), and as the student begins pantomiming, repeat the term over and over again ("<u>Wo shi jingcha</u>," "<u>wo shi jingcha</u>"...), until the class guesses the definition and states it in English. Repeat the statement "<u>Wo shi jingcha</u>," and have the entire class make the gesture that finally made them realize what was being mimed. Ask them to state the term, and then proceed to another term, using the same or a different volunteer. When you have gone through all the terms to be introduced, review by stating each of the terms in turn, and having the students demonstrate comprehension simply by miming its meaning. Finally, you mime the terms, and have the students state them in Chinese.

Pantomiming is convenient since the teacher does not need to prepare props for it: the students are the props, and they generally enjoy both putting on a show themselves, and watching their classmates perform.

2.15   Picture-cards

Another way of drilling new material is to pass out picture cards (either those provided in this volume or others cut from magazines, etc.) that illustrate new vocabulary, one each to the students. (Duplicate copies of pictures are fine; then more than one student would have any particular picture.) They hold the pictures so as to make them clearly visible to all. *Pinyin* for the term illustrated by the picture is written inconspicuously on the back of the picture, so that only the student holding it knows how the term is said in Chinese. Then as the teacher either names the items, or makes statements or asks questions that refers to each item, the student holding the picture raises it up. After a round or two, have the students exchange their pictures. Repeat another round or two. When students begin to demonstrate some familiarity with the material, check comprehension by asking the class as a whole to point to a picture, upon your cue.

You may also eventually wish to ask a volunteer student to take over your role, and provide the cues for the class.

2.16   Visiting

The students sit in a square or circle as best they can, space permitting. Ask four or five students at a time (spaced across the circle so that there are several students between them) to get up and make their way clockwise around the circle, carrying out a task with each student she comes to. These are generally very "quick and dirty" tasks, such as "Identify and greet the person (<u>Wang yisheng, nin hao; Zhang nüshi, nin hao; Xiao Li, ni hao</u>)." When the student reaches her own seat, she sits down and another student can then get up and begin his rounds.

3.   Characteristics of this curriculum

<u>Communicating in Chinese</u> consists of 2 volumes, listening/speaking and reading/ writing, with a student text and teachers' guide for each. The materials are intended to support but not prescribe the progress of teaching and learning in and out of the classroom. There is no standard classroom, class, or teacher—people and settings are as different as they are alike. Teaching and learning proceed at varied paces and in various fashions, depending on the needs, motivation, ability, and learning styles of the students; the language/instructional background, the instructional style, the motivation and the personality of the teacher; the administrative framework in which instruction is provided; types and variety of teaching materials available; the amount of support provided by the community, etc. In the final analysis, the quality of instruction and of learning depend almost entirely on the strength of the teacher and the students, rather than on the text or the teaching methodology used.

Effective teachers can teach using almost any text (although the degree to which they may be hampered by the text varies), and they will find effective methods of training their students. Skillful students will find a way to learn in almost any context, although again the style and content of instruction may facilitate or impede their learning. Conversely, the most inspired text or methodology will flounder in the hands of an uninspired teacher.

The goal of <u>Communicating in Chinese</u> is to, as much as possible, facilitate rather than hamper the teacher's instructional style and the student's learning style. The curriculum is intended to be agglutinative rather than monolithic: pieces can be added or left out here and there without harm to the integrity of the whole. Teachers are encouraged to add, delete, and modify as necessary.

The suggested activities for each lesson included in this volume begin with "skills-getting" activities: introduction, comprehension drills, and oral practice, and are followed by "skills-using" activities: controlled use. The difference between a drill and a practice activity is simply one of degree: drills are more mechanical, focus more on discrete forms, and require less creative use of language than do the practice activities. Controlled use activities make greater demands on the students' total language resources, and require the students to make decisions about which language forms are appropriate to use in particular situations.

4. Syllabus planning

4.1 Goals & Objectives

Based on previous experience in testing students at the end of a semester and year, I decided that, for my class, Novice High in all four skills would be a reasonable goal for the first semester of instruction (based on approximately 60 contact hours), and Intermediate Low would be reasonable for the end of the second semester (for a total instruction time of 120 hours). By contrast, the Chinese section of the University of Hawaii's 1991 Summer Institute for Foreign Language Teachers, sponsored by the National Foreign Language Resource Center at Hawaii, concurred on the following goals for 50 hours of instruction: Listening: Intermediate Low; Speaking: Novice High; Reading: Intermediate Low; Writing: Novice High. You will need to adjust the goals for your own students. In any case, it would be useful to include a statement such as the following (which is based on a goal of Novice High) on the course description sheet, to let your students know what to expect from the course.

4.1.1 Semester one

Students will gain listening, speaking, reading and writing skills in standard (Mandarin) Chinese, attaining approximately the Novice High level on the ACTFL proficiency scale. Specifically, students will be able to achieve the following abilities.

Listening   Able to understand short. learned utterances and some sentence-length utterances, expecially where context supports understanding and speech is clear. Comprehends limited vocabulary and some simple questions/statements about family members, age, address, time, daily activities, interests, needs, and shopping.

Speaking   Emerging ability to make short statements and ask simple questions, primarily by relying on memorized utterances but occasionally by expanding these through simple recombinations of their elements. Vocabulary centers on areas such as common objects, places, activities, basic likes and dislikes, terms for immediate family members.

Reading   Can identify a limited number of character components and high-frequency characters in areas of immediate need. Where specific characters and combinations have been memorized, can read for instructional and directional purposes standardized messages, such as some items on menus, prices in stores, time/date on schedules, and simple public instructions.

Writing   *Able to write simple fixed expressions and limited memorized material and some recombinations thereof. Can supply information on simple forms and documents. Can write names, numbers, dates, own nationality, and other simple autobiographical information as well as some short phrases and simple lists.*

4.1.1   second semester

Students will gain listening, speaking, reading and writing skills in standard (Mandarin) Chinese, attaining approximately the Intermediate Low level on the ACTFL proficiency scale. Specifically, students will be able to achieve the following.

Listening   *Able to understand sentence-length utterances which consist of recombinations of learned elements in a limited number of content areas, particularly if strongly supported by the situational context. Comprehension areas include such basic needs as getting meals, lodging, and transportation, and receiving simple instructions and routine commands.*

Speaking   *Able to handle successfully a limited number of uncomplicated task-oriented and social functions. Can ask and answer questions, initiate and respond to simple statements and maintain face-to-face conversation. Can perform such tasks as introducing self, ordering a meal, asking directions, and making purchases.*

Reading   *Can read, for basic survival and social needs, simple connected, specially prepared material and can puzzle out pieces of some authentic material with considerable difficulty, as it reflects similarity to specially prepared material and/or to high-frequency oral vocabulary and structure. Can puzzle out, with difficulty and frequent error, very simple hand-printed messages, personal notes and very short letters which are written by a native speaker used to dealing with foreigners. Able to decode one or two elements from simplest connected texts dealing with basic personal and social needs, such as signs, public announcements and short, straightforward instructions dealing with public life.*

Writing   *Able to meet limited practical writing needs. Can write short messages, postcards, and take down simple notes, such as telephone messages. Can create statements or questions within the scope of limited language experience. Material produced consists of recombinations of learned vocabulary and structures into simple sentences on very familiar topics.*

Subsequently, you might rough out a course syllabus by spiraling in selected activities in succession. Beginning with Unit 1, you might first introduce the new material (see suggestions for introducing Unit 1), then provide an opportunity for meaningful drill (see suggestions for drilling Unit 1), next provide an opportunity for communicative practice (see suggestions for practicing Unit 1), and finally provide an opportunity for situational use (see suggestions for controlled use of Unit 1). You may not need to cover every step: your students may pick up the material quickly enough for you to skip a step or two, in which case it would be better to skip either drill or practice than to skip controlled use. On the other hand, you may find that the suggestions given in this manual are insufficient, and may need to add more meaningful drill, communicative practice, or situational use exercises. Later you might want to spiral in the reading and writing activities (see volume II).

Do keep the following points in mind when developing your syllabus.

1) Variety and work with smaller, more learnable units of work will prove to be of greater benefit to your students than material presented in a single long string. In other words, it is better to break up Unit 1 over several days, say introducing it on day 1, drilling it on day 2 (and beginning Unit 2 on day 2), practicing it on day 3 (and drilling Unit 2 and beginning Unit 3 on day 2), doing controlled use on day 4 (and practicing Unit 2 and drilling Unit 3 on day 3), and beginning reading and writing sometime later, than to devote day 1 to all activities related to Unit 1, day 2 to all activities related to Unit 2, day 3 to all activities related to Unit 3, etc.

2) In keeping with the idea of varying activities, each activity you present will likely not take any longer than, at the maximum, 10-15 minutes. Some may be as brief as 2-3 minutes. Therefore, for each class period you will want to plan several activities, say 4-5 activities for a 50 minute class period.

3) If you teach all four skills, you may want to try to include some work on each skill every day.

4) Don't forget to include time for divergent activities every so often, to "take the measure" of your student's developing proficiencies.

4.2 Sample syllabi

Following is a sample course outline that was used in a Chinese 101 four-skills class at the University of Hawaii, meeting Monday through Friday, 55 minutes per day. The original outline planned for the introduction of some supplementary reading (The Heartless Husband, PALI reading series, University of Hawaii Press) towards the end of the semester, but in implementation this reading was forfeited to allow for additional review and integrative activities. When a unit number is mentioned (e.g. "Unit 2g"), reference is to Volume 1: the listening/speaking textbook. A unit number followed by "-r" (e.g. "Unit 2g-r") refers to reading activities in Volume 2, and a unit number followed by "-w" (e.g. "Unit 2g-w") refers to writing activities in Volume 2. The column labelled "Lab" lists the call numbers for the appropriate audiotapes that were available in the language laboratory. You will, of course, need to make arrangements with your own audio-visual support services if you wish to provide audiotape support to your students.

4.2.1 Sample first semester syllabus

Date	Procedures	Lab	Homework	Content
M 8/27	Intro #s 0-10. Goals & objectives of class. #s 0-10 in characters	CB 400.1	Look through textbk.	numbers names student names.
T 8/28	Student names. #s 0-100. Intro Unit 1. Classroom expressions.	CB 400.1 CB 401.1	Write #1-10. Write own surname.	numbers names Unit 1 Class exps.
W 8/29	Student names. #s 0-10,000.	CB 400.1 CB 401.1	Tang poetry: initials & tones.	numbers names

	Drill Unit 1. Pinyin practice. Classroom expressions.			pinyin Class exps. Unit 1
Th 8/30	Student names. #drills. Brainstorm Unit 1. Pinyin practice. Classroom expressions.	CB 400.1 CB 401.1	Tang poetry: initials & tones.	pinyin numbers Unit 1 Class exps.
F 8/31	Student names. # practice. Practice Unit 1. Pinyin practice. Classroom expressions.	CB 400.1 CB 401.1	Tang poetry: finals & tones. Unit 1: Dial. prac.	pinyin numbers Unit 1
M 9/3	HOLIDAY (Labor Day)			
T 9/4	Use Unit 1. Intro Unit 2a Drill Unit 2a Unit 1: Dial. prac. Pinyin practice.	CB 401.1 CB 402.1	Tang poetry: finals & tones	pinyin Unit 1 Unit 2a
W 9/5	Brainstorm Unit 2a Practice Unit 2a Use Unit 2a TEST: pinyin, #s, Unit 1	CB 402.1	Unit 2a: dial. prac. Tang poetry: transcription	pinyin Unit 1 Unit 2a
Th 9/6	Unit 2a: dial. prac. Intro/drill Unit 2b Pinyin practice.	CB 402.1 CB 402.2	Tang poetry: transcription	Unit 2b
F 9/7	Brainstorm Unit 2b Practice Unit 2b Pinyin practice.	CB 402.2	Unit 2b: dial. prac. Transcription.	Unit 2b
M 9/10	Unit 2b: dial. prac. Intro/drill Unit 2c Intro radicals	CB 402.2 CB 402.3	radicals	Unit 2c Radicals
T 9/11	Practice Unit 2c Use Unit 2c Intro radicals	CB 402.3	radicals Unit 2c: dial. prac.	Unit 2c Radicals
W 9/12	Intro/drill Unit 2d Intro/drill Unit 1-reading Unit 2c: dial. prac.	CB 402.4	Unit 1: read. drill	Unit 2d Unit 1-r
Th 9/13	Practice Unit 2d Practice Unit 1-reading Intro/drill Unit 1-writing TEST: Units 2a, b, c; radicals	CB 402.4	Unit 2d: dial. prac.	Unit 2d Unit 1-r Unit 1-w

F 9/14	Use Unit 2d Unit 2c: dial. prac. Use Unit 1-reading Intro/drill Unit 1-writing	CB 402.4		Unit 2d Unit 1-r Unit 1-w
M 9/17	Intro/drill Unit 2e Intro/drill Unit 2a-reading Intro/drill Unit 1-writing	CB 402.5	Unit 2a: read. drill	Unit 2e Unit 2a-r Unit 1-w
T 9/18	Practice Unit 2e Practice Unit 2a-reading Practice Unit 1-writing	CB 402.5	Unit 2e: dial. prac.	Unit 2e Unit 2a-r Unit 1-w
W 9/19	Use Unit 2e Unit 2e: dial. prac. Use Unit 2a-reading Practice Unit 1-writing	CB 402.5		Unit 2e Unit 2a-r Unit 1-w
Th 9/20	Intro/drill Unit 2f Intro/drill Unit 2b-reading Use writing TEST: Units 2d, e; 1-r, 2a-r	CB 402.6	Unit 2b: read. drill	Unit 2f Unit 2b-r Unit 1-w
F 9/21	Practice Unit 2f Practice Unit 2b-reading	CB 402.6	Unit 2f: dial. prac.	Unit 2f
M 9/24	Use Unit 2f Unit 2f: dial. prac. Use Unit 2b-reading Intro/drill Unit 2a-writing	CB 402.6		Unit 2f Unit 2b-r Unit 2a-w
T 9/25	Intro/drill Unit 2g Intro/drill Unit 2a-writing Use writing	CB 402.7		Unit 2g Unit 2b-r Unit 2a-w
W 9/26	Practice Unit 2g Intro/drill Unit 2c-reading Unit 2g: dial. prac. Practice Unit 2a-writing	CB 402.7	Unit 2g: dial. prac. Unit 2c: read. drill	Unit 2g Unit 2c-r Unit 2a-w
Th 9/27	Use Unit 2g Practice Unit 2c-reading TEST: Unit 2f; 2b-r; 1-w	CB 402.7		Unit 2g Unit 2c-r
F 9/28	Intro/drill Unit 2h Use Unit 2c-reading Intro/drill Unit 2b-writing	CB 402.8		Unit 2h Unit 2c-r Unit 2b-w
M 10/1	Practice Unit 2h Intro/drill Unit 2d-reading Unit 2h: dial. prac.	CB 402.8	Unit 2h: dial. prac. Unit 2d: read. drill	Unit 2h Unit 2d-r

	Practice Unit 2b-writing			Unit 2b-w
T 10/2	Use Unit 2h Practice Unit 2d-reading Use writing	CB 402.8	Unit 1: struc. notes	Unit 2h Unit 2d-r Unit 2b-w
W 10/3	Intro/drill Unit 3a Use Unit 2d-reading Unit 1: struc. notes	CB 403.1		Unit 3a Unit 2d-r
Th 10/4	Practice Unit 3a Intro/drill Unit 2e-reading Intro/drill Unit 2c-writing TEST: Units 2g, 2h; 2c-r, 2d-r; 2a-w, 2b-w	CB 403.1	Unit 3a: dial. prac. Unit 2e: read. drill Unit 2a: struc. notes	Unit 3a Unit 2e-r Unit 2c-w
F 10/5	Use Unit 3a Unit 3a: dial. prac. Practice Unit 2e-reading Practice Unit 2c-writing Unit 2a: struc. notes	CB 403.1		Unit 3a Unit 2e-r Unit 2c-w
M 10/8	Intro/drill Unit 3b Use Unit 2e-reading Use writing	CB 403.2	Unit 2b: struc. notes	Unit 3b Unit 2e-r Unit 2c-w
T 10/9	Practice Unit 3b Intro/drill Unit 2f-reading Unit 2b: struc. notes	CB 403.2	Unit 3b: dial. prac. Unit 2f: read. drill	Unit 3b Unit 2f-r
W 10/10	Use Unit 3b Unit 3b: dial. prac. Practice Unit 2f-reading Intro/drill Unit 2d-writing	CB 403.2	Unit 2c: struc. notes	Unit 3b Unit 2f-r Unit 2d-w
Th 10/11	Intro/drill Unit 4a Use Unit 2f-reading Intro/drill Unit 2d-writing Unit 2c: struc. notes	CB 404.1		Unit 4a Unit 2f-r Unit 2d-w
F 10/12	Practice Unit 4a Intro/drill Unit 2g-reading Practice Unit 2d-writing TEST: Units 3a, 3b; 2e-r, 2f-r; 2c-w	CB 404.1	Unit 4a: dial. prac. Unit 2g: read. drill Unit 2d: struc. notes	Unit 4a Unit 2g-r Unit 2d-w
M 10/15	Use Unit 4a Unit 4a: dial. prac. Practice Unit 2g-reading Use writing Unit 2d: struc. notes	CB 404.1		Unit 4a Unit 2g-r Unit 2d-w
T 10/16	Intro/drill Unit 4b Use Unit 2g-reading	CB 404.2	Unit 2e: struc. notes	Unit 4b Unit 2g-r

W 10/17	Practice Unit 4b Intro/drill Unit 2h-reading Intro/drill Unit 2f-writing Unit 2e: struc. notes	CB 404.2	Unit 4b: dial. prac. Unit 2h: read. drill	Unit 4b Unit 2h-r Unit 2f-w
Th 10/18	Use Unit 4b Unit 4b: dial. prac. Practice Unit 2h-reading Practice Unit 2f-writing	CB 404.2	Unit 2f: struc. notes	Unit 4b Unit 2h-r Unit 2f-w
F 10/19	Intro/drill Unit 4c Use Unit 2h-reading Unit 2f: struc. notes TEST: 4a, 4b; 2g-r; 2d-w, 2f-w	CB 404.3		Unit 4c Unit 2h-r
M 10/22	Practice Unit 4c Intro/drill Unit 3a-reading Intro/drill Unit 2g-writing	CB 404.3	Unit 4c: dial. prac. Unit 3a: read. drill Unit 2g: struc. notes	Unit 4c Unit 3a-r Unit 2g-w
T 10/23	Use Unit 4c Unit 4c: dial. prac. Practice Unit 3a-reading Practice Unit 2g-writing Unit 2g: struc. notes	CB 404.3		Unit 4c Unit 3a-r Unit 2g-w
W 10/24	Intro/drill Unit 4d Use Unit 3a-reading Use writing	CB 404.4	Unit 3a: struc. notes	Unit 4d Unit 3a-r Unit 2g-w
Th 10/25	Practice Unit 4d Intro/drill Unit 3b-reading Unit 3a: struc. notes TEST: 4c; 2h-r, 3a-r; 2g-w	CB 404.4	Unit 4d: dial. prac. Unit 3b: read. drill	Unit 4d Unit 3b-r
F 10/26	Use Unit 4d Unit 4d: dial. prac. Practice Unit 3b-reading Intro/drill Unit 2h-writing	CB 404.4	Unit 3b: struc. notes	Unit 4d Unit 3b-r Unit 2h-w
M 10/29	Intro/drill Unit 4e Use Unit 3b-reading Practice Unit 2h-writing Unit 3b: struc. notes	CB 404.5		Unit 4e Unit 3b-r Unit 2h-w
T 10/30	HOLIDAY (Election Day)			
W 10/31	Practice Unit 4e Intro/drill Unit 4a-reading Use writing	CB 404.5	Unit 4e: dial. prac. Unit 4a: read. drill	Unit 4e Unit 4a-r Unit 2h-w
Th 11/1	Use Unit 4e Unit 4e: dial. prac. Practice Unit 4a-reading	CB 404.5	Unit 4a: struc. notes	Unit 4e Unit 4a-r

TEST: 4d; 3b-r; 2h-w

F 11/2	Intro/drill Unit 5a Unit 4a: struc. notes Use Unit 4a-reading Intro/drill Unit 3a-writing	CB 405.1		Unit 5a Unit 4a-r Unit 3a-w
M 11/5	Practice Unit 5a Intro/drill Unit 4b-reading Practice Unit 3a-writing	CB 405.1	Unit 5a: dial. prac. Unit 4b: read. drill	Unit 5a Unit 4b-r Unit 3a-w
T 11/6	Use Unit 5a Unit 5a: dial. prac. Practice Unit 4b-reading	CB 405.1	Unit 4b: struc. notes	Unit 5a Unit 4b-r
W 11/7	Intro/drill Unit 5b Unit 4b: struc. notes Use Unit 4b-reading Intro/drill Unit 3b-writing	CB 405.2		Unit 5b Unit 4b-r Unit 3b-w
Th 11/8	Practice Unit 5b Intro/drill Unit 5a-reading Practice Unit 3b-writing	CB 405.2	Unit 5b: dial. prac. Unit 5a: read. drill	Unit 5b Unit 5a-r Unit 3b-w
F 11/9	Use Unit 5b Unit 5b: dial. prac. Practice Unit 5a-reading Use writing	CB 405.2	Unit 4c: struc. notes	Unit 5b Unit 5a-r Unit 3b-w
M 11/12	HOLIDAY (Veteran's Day)			
T 11/13	Intro/drill Unit 5c Unit 4c: struc. notes Use Unit 5a-reading TEST: 4e, 5a, 5b; 4a-r, 4b-r; 3a-w, 3b-w	CB 405.3		Unit 5c Unit 5a-r
W 11/14	Practice Unit 5c Intro/drill Unit 5b-reading Intro/drill Unit 4a-writing	CB 405.3	Unit 5c: dial. prac. Unit 5b: read. drill	Unit 5c Unit 5b-r Unit 4a-w
Th 11/15	Use Unit 5c Unit 5c: dial. prac. Practice Unit 5b-reading Practice Unit 4a-writing	CB 405.3	Unit 4d: struc. notes	Unit 5c Unit 5b-r Unit 4a-w
F 11/16	Intro/drill Unit 5d Unit 4d: struc. notes Use Unit 5b-reading	CB 405.4		Unit 5d Unit 5b-r

M 11/19	Practice Unit 5d Intro/drill Unit 5c-reading Intro/drill Unit 4b-writing TEST: 5c; 5a-r, 5b-r; 4a-w	CB 405.4	Unit 5d: dial. prac. Unit 5c: read. drill	Unit 5d Unit 5c-r Unit 4b-w
T 11/20	Use Unit 5d Unit 5d: dial. prac. Practice Unit 5c-reading Practice Unit 4b-writing	CB 405.4	Unit 4e: struc. notes	Unit 5d Unit 5c-r Unit 4b-w
W 11/21	Intro/drill Unit 5e Unit 4e: struc. notes Use Unit 5c-reading Use writing	CB 405.5		Unit 5e Unit 5c-r Unit 4b-w
Th 11/22	HOLIDAY (Thanksgiving Day)			
F 11/23	HOLIDAY (Non-instructional Day)			

M 11/26	Practice Unit 5e Intro/drill Unit 5d-reading	CB 405.5	Unit 5e: dial. prac. Unit 5d: read. drill	Unit 5e Unit 5d-r
T 11/27	Use Unit 5e Unit 5e: dial. prac. Practice Unit 5d-reading Intro/drill Unit 5a-writing	CB 405.5	Unit 5a: struc. notes	Unit 5e Unit 5d-r Unit 5a-w
W 11/28	Intro/drill Unit 6a Unit 5a: struc. notes Use Unit 5d-reading Practice Unit 5a-writing	CB 406.1	Unit 5b: struc. notes	Unit 6a Unit 5d-r Unit 5a-w
Th 11/29	Practice Unit 6a Intro/drill Unit 5e-reading Unit 5b: struc. notes TEST: 5d, 5e; 5c-r, 5d-r; 4b-w, 5a-w	CB 406.1	Unit 6a: dial. prac. Unit 5e: read. drill	Unit 6a Unit 5e-r
F 11/30	Use Unit 6a Unit 6a: dial. prac. Practice Unit 5e-reading Intro/drill Unit 5b-writing	CB 406.1	Unit 6a: struc. notes	Unit 6a Unit 5e-r Unit 5b-w

---

M 12/3	Intro/drill Unit 6b Unit 6a: struc. notes Use Unit 5e-reading Practice Unit 5b-writing	CB 406.2		Unit 6b Unit 5e-r Unit 5b-w
T 12/4	Practice Unit 6b Intro/drill Unit 6a-reading Divergent activity	CB 406.2	Unit 6b: dial. prac. Unit 6a: read. drill	Unit 6b Unit 6a-r
W 12/5	Use Unit 6b Unit 6b: dial. prac.	CB 406.2		Unit 6b

	Practice Unit 6a-reading		Unit 6a-r
	Intro/drill Unit 5c-writing		Unit 5c-w
Th 12/6	Role play	Unit 6b: struc. notes	Review
	Use Unit 6a-reading		Unit 6a-r
	Practice Unit 5c-writing		Unit 5c-w
	TEST: 6a, 6b; 5e-r; 5b-w		
F 12/7	Role play		
	Unit 6b: struc. notes		
	Intro/drill Unit 6b-reading	Unit 6b: read. drill	Unit 6b-r
	Intro/drill Unit 5e-writing		Unit 5e-w
M 12/10	Role play		
	Practice Unit 6b-reading		Unit 6b-r
	Use writing		
T 12/11	Role play		
	Use Unit 6b-reading		Unit 6b-r
W 12/12	Review & summation		

4.2.2   Sample second semester syllabus

For the second semester, some adjustments were made in the format of the syllabus: notably, explicit instructions to work on the Dialog, Grammar notes, and Culture Notes segments of the text were added. I also introduced a supplementary narrative text. Laughing in Chinese by Peggy Wang (Sodilis, 1986) was used with good results.

Class Schedule

Date	*Procedures*	*Lab*	*Homework*	*Content*
M 1/14	review 101 exam learn zhao pengyou (a song) Student names	review	review 101 chars.	review pinyin names
T 1/15	review activities Laugh 1 (t/n)	CB 406.1	preview 6a Laugh 1 (shuo)	review READER
W 1/16	Intro 6a Laugh 1 (sh)	CB 406.1	6a vocabulary Laugh 1 (xiang/xie)	Unit 6a READER
Th 1/17	Drill 6a Laugh 1 (overview) Laugh 2 (t/n)	CB 406.1	6a dialogues Laugh 2 (shuo)	Unit 6a READER
F 1/18	Use 6a 6a dialogues Laugh 2 (sh)	CB 406.1 CB 406.2	6a "A poster" & culture notes preview 6b Laugh 2 (xiang/xie)	Unit 6a READER

M 1/21	HOLIDAY (Martin Luther King Day)			
T 1/22	TEST: 6a, L1 Intro 6b Laugh 2 (overview)	CB 406.1 CB 406.2	6b vocabulary	Unit 6b READER
W 1/23	Drill 6b Intro 6a-R Laugh 3 (t/n)	CB 406.2	6b dialogues 6a-R vocabulary Laugh 3 (shuo)	Unit 6b Unit 6a-R READER
Th 1/24	Use 6b 6b dialogues Prac 6a-R Intro 6a-W	CB 406.2	6b "After the poster" & culture notes 6a-W vocabulary	Unit 6b Unit 6a-R Unit 6a-W
F 1/25	Divergent activity Prac 6a-W Laugh 3 (sh)	CB 407.1	preview 7a Laugh 3 (xiang/xie)	READER
M 1/28	TEST: 6b, 6a-R, 6a-W, L2 Intro 7a Laugh 3 (overview)	CB 407.1	7a vocabulary 6a structural exercise	Unit 7a Unit 6a READER
T 1/29	Drill 7a 6a structure Intro 6b-R Laugh 4 (t/n)	CB 407.1	7a dialogues 6b-R vocabulary Laugh 4 (shuo)	Unit 7a Unit 6a Unit 6b-R READER
W 1/30	Use 7a 7a dialogues Prac 6b-R Laugh 4 (sh)	CB 407.2	7a "Visiting Zhang" & culture notes preview 7b Laugh 4 (xiang/xie)	Unit 7a Unit 6b-R READER
Th 1/31	Intro 7b Intro 6b-W Laugh 4 (overview)	CB 407.2	7b vocabulary 6b structural exercise 6b-W vocabulary	Unit 7b Unit 6b Unit 6b-W
F 2/1	Drill 7b 6b structure Intro 7a-R Prac 6b-W	CB 407.2	7b dialogues 7a-R vocabulary	Unit 7b Unit 7a-R Unit 6b-W
M 2/4	TEST: 7a, 6b-R, 6b-W, L3/4 Use 7b	CB 407.2 CB 407.3	7b "Privacy" & culture notes preview 7c	Unit 7b
T 2/5	7b dialogues Intro 7c Prac 7a-R Laugh 5 (t/n)	CB 407.3	7c vocabulary 7a structural exercise Laugh 5 (shuo)	Unit 7c Unit 7a Unit 7a-R READER
W 2/6	Drill 7c 7a structure Intro 7a-W Laugh 5 (sh)	CB 407.3	7c dialogues 7a-W vocabulary Laugh 5 (xiang/xie)	Unit 7c Unit 7a-W READER

Th 2/7	Use 7c 7c dialogues Intro 7b-R Prac 7a-W	CB 407.3 CB 407.4	preview 7d 7b-R vocabulary	Unit 7c Unit 7b-R Unit 7a-W
F 2/8	Intro/drill 7d Prac 7b-R Intro 7b-W Laugh 5 (overview)	CB 407.4 READER	7d vocabulary 7b structural exercise 7b-W vocabulary	Unit 7d Unit 7b Unit 7b-R Unit 7b-W
M 2/11	TEST: 7b/c; 7a/b-R; 7a-W; L5 7b structure	CB 407.4	7d dialogues	Unit 7d Unit 7b
T 2/12	Use 7d 7d dialogues Intro 7c-R Laugh 6 (t/n)	CB 407.4	7d "Morning routines" & cult notes 7c-R vocabulary Laugh 6 (shuo)	Unit 7d Unit 7c-R Unit 7b-W READER
W 2/13	Divergent activity Prac 7c-R Prac 7b-W Laugh 6 (sh)	CB 408.1	preview 8a Laugh 6 (xiang/xie)	Unit 7c-R READER
Th 2/14	Intro 8a Intro 7c-W Laugh 6 (overview)	CB 408.1	8a vocabulary 7c structural exercise 7c-W vocabulary	Unit 8a Unit 7c Unit 7c-W READER
F 2/15	Drill 8a 7c structure Laugh 7 (t/n) Prac 7c-W	CB 408.1	8a "Cleaning the classroom" & culture notes Laugh 7 (shuo)	Unit 8a READER Unit 7c-W
M 2/18	HOLIDAY (Presidents' Day)			
T 2/19	TEST:7d; 7c-R; 7b-W; L6 Use 8a	CB 408.1 CB 408.2	8a dialogues preview 8b	Unit 8a
W 2/20	8a dialogues Intro 8b Intro 7d-R Laugh 7 (sh)	CB 408.1 CB 408.2	8b vocabulary 7d structural exercise 7d-R vocabulary Laugh 7 (xiang/xie)	Unit 8b Unit 7d Unit 7d-R READER
Th 2/21	Drill 8b 7d structure Prac 7d-R Laugh 7 (overview)	CB 408.2	8b dialogues	Unit 8b Unit 7d Unit 7d-R READER
F 2/22	Use Unit 8b 8b dialogues Intro 7d-W Laugh 8 (t/n)	CB 408.2 CB 408.3	8b "Plans" & culture notes preview 8c 7d-W vocabulary Laugh 8 (shuo)	Unit 8b Unit 7d-W READER

M 2/25	TEST:8a/b; 7d-R;7c-W;L7 Intro 8c	CB 408.3	8c vocabulary 8a structural exercise	Unit 8c Unit 8a
T 2/26 Intro 8a-R	Drill 8c 8a structure Prac 7d-W	CB 408.3	8c dialogues 8a-R vocabulary Unit 8a-R	Unit 8c Unit 8a Unit 7d-W
W 2/27	Use 8c 8c dialogues Prac 8a-R Laugh 8 (sh)	CB 408.3 CB 408.4	8c "Looking for David" & cult. notes preview 8d Laugh 8 (xiang/xie)	Unit 8c Unit 8a-R READER
Th 2/28	Intro 8d Intro 8a-W Laugh 8 (overview) Laugh 9 (t/n)	CB 408.4	8d vocabulary 8b structural exercise 8a-W vocabulary	Unit 8d Unit 8b Unit 8a-W READER
F 3/1	Drill 8d 8b structure Intro 8b-R Prac 8a-W	CB 408.4	8d "Gossip" & culture notes 8b-R vocabulary	Unit 8d Unit 8b-R Unit 8a-W
M 3/4	TEST:8c; 8a-R; 7d/8a-W; L8 Use 8d	CB 408.4	8d dialogues Laugh 9 (shuo)	Unit 8d
T 3/5	8d dialogues Divergent activity Prac 8b-R Laugh 9 (sh)	CB 408.4 CB 409.1	preview 9a Laugh 9 (xiang/xie)	Unit 8d Unit 8b-R READER
W 3/6	Intro 9a Intro 8b-W Laugh 9 (overview) Laugh 10 (t/n)	CB 409.1	9a vocabulary 8c structural exercise 8b-W vocabulary	Unit 9a Unit 8c Unit 8b-W READER
Th 3/7	Drill 9a 8c structure Intro 8c-R Prac 8b-W	CB 409.1	9a dialogues 8c-R vocabulary Laugh 10 (shuo)	Unit 9a Unit 8c Unit 8c-R Unit 8b-W
F 3/8	Use 9a 9a dialogues Prac 8c-R Laugh 10 (sh)	CB 409.1 CB 409.2	9a "Food for dinner" & culture notes preview 9b Laugh 10 (xiang/xie)	Unit 9a Unit 8c-R READER
M 3/11	TEST:8d/9a; 8b/c-R; 8b-W;L9 Intro 9b Laugh 10 (overview)	CB 409.2	9b vocabulary 8d structural exercise	Unit 9b Unit 8d
T 3/12	Drill 9b 8d structure Intro 8d-R Intro 8c-W	CB 409.2	9b dialogues 8d-R vocabulary 8c-W vocabulary	Unit 9b Unit 8d Unit 8d-R Unit 8c-W

W 3/13	Use 9b 9b dialogues Prac 8d-R Prac 8c-W	CB 409.2 CB 409.3	9b "Eating out" & culture notes preview 9c	Unit 9b Unit 8d-R Unit 8c-W
Th 3/14	Intro 9c Intro 8d-W Laugh 11 (t/n)	CB 409.3	9c vocabulary 9a structural exercise 8d-W vocabulary Laugh 11 (shuo)	Unit 9c Unit 9a Unit 8d-W READER
F 3/15	Drill 9c 9a structure Prac 8d-W Laugh 11 (sh)	CB 409.3	9c "Eating out" & culture notes Laugh 11 (xiang/xie)	Unit 9c Unit 9a Unit 8d-W READER
M 3/18	TEST:9b; 8d-R;8c/d-W;L10 Use 9c Laugh 11 (overview)	CB 409.3 CB 409.4	9c dialogues preview 9d	Unit 9c READER
T 3/19	9c dialogues Intro 9d Intro 9a-R Laugh 12 (t/n)	CB 409.4	9d vocabulary 9b structural exercise 9a-R vocabulary Laugh 12 (shuo)	Unit 9d Unit 9b Unit 9a-R READER
W 3/20	Drill 9d 9b structure Prac 9a-R Laugh 12 (sh)	CB 409.4	9d dialogues Laugh 12 (xiang/xie)	Unit 9d Unit 9b Unit 9a-R READER
Th 3/21	Use 9d 9d dialogues Intro 9a-W Laugh 12 (overview)	CB 409.4	9d "Eating Western style" & culture notes 9a-W vocabulary	Unit 9d Unit 9a-W READER
F 3/22	Divergent activity Intro 9b-R Prac 9a-W Laugh 13 (t/n)	CB 409.4 CB 410.1	review preview 10a 9b-R vocabulary Laugh 13 (shuo)	Unit 9b-R Unit 9a-W READER

SPRING BREAK

M 4/1	TEST:9c/d;9a-R;9a-W;L11/12 Intro10a	CB 410.1	10a vocabulary 9c structural exercise	Unit 10a Unit 9c
T 4/2	Drill 10a 9c structure Prac 9b-R Laugh 13 (sh)	CB 410.1	10a dialogues Laugh 13 (xiang/xie)	Unit 10a Unit 9c Unit 9b-R READER
W 4/3	Use 10a 10a dialogues Intro 9b-W Laugh 13 (overview)	CB 410.1 CB 410.2	10a "Visitors" & culture notes preview 10b 9b-W vocabulary	Unit 10a Unit 9b-W READER

Day	Activity	CB	Assignment	Unit
Th 4/4	Intro 10b Prac 9b-W Laugh 14 (t/n)	CB 410.2	10b vocabulary 9d structural exercise Laugh 14 (shuo)	Unit 10b Unit 9d Unit 9b-W READER
F 4/5	Drill 10b 9d structure Intro 9c-R Laugh 14 (sh)	CB 410.2	10b "David's parents" & c. notes 9c-R vocabulary Laugh 14 (xiang/xie)	Unit 10b Unit 9c-R READER
M 4/8	TEST:10a;9b-R;9b-W;L13 Use 10b Laugh 14 (overview)		10b dialogues preview 10c	Unit 10b READER
T 4/9	10b dialogues Intro 10c Prac 9c-R Intro 9c-W	CB 410.2 CB 410.3	10c vocabulary 10a structural exercise 9c-W vocabulary	Unit 10c Unit 10a Unit 9c-R Unit 9c-W
W 4/10	Drill 10c 10a structure Prac 9c-W Laugh 15 (t/n)	CB 410.3	10c dialogues Laugh 15 (shuo)	Unit 10c Unit 10a Unit 9c-W READER
Th 4/11	Use 10c 10c dialogues Intro 9d-R Laugh 15 (sh)	CB 410.3 CB 410.4	10c "Finding P.O." & culture notes preview 10d 9d-R vocabulary Laugh 15 (xiang/xie)	Unit 10c Unit 9d-R READER
F 4/12	Intro 10d Prac 9d-R Laugh 15 (overview) Laugh 16 (t/n)	CB 410.4	10d vocabulary Laugh 16 (shuo)	Unit 10d Unit 9d-R READER
M 4/15	TEST:10b/c; 9c/d-R;9c-W;L14/15 Drill 10d	CB 410.4	10d dialogues 10b structural exercise	Unit 10d Unit 10b
T 4/16	Use 10d 10d dialogues 10b structure Intro 9d-W	CB 410.4 CB 410.5	10d "Travel asp" & c. notes preview 10e 9d-W vocabulary	Unit 10d Unit 10b Unit 9d-W
W 4/17	Intro 10e Intro 10a-R Prac 9d-W Laugh 16 (sh)	CB 410.5	10e vocabulary 10a-R vocabulary 10c structural exercise Laugh 16 (xiang/xie)	Unit 10e Unit 10a-R Unit 10c Unit 9d-W READER
Th 4/18	Drill 10e 10c structure Prac 10a-R Laugh 16 (overview)	CB 410.5	10e dialogues	Unit 10e Unit 10c Unit 10a-R READER

F 4/19	Use 10e 10e dialogues Intro 10a-W Laugh 17 (t/n)	CB 410.5	10e "Farewell" & culture notes 10a-W vocabulary	Unit 10e Unit 10a-W READER
M 4/22	TEST:10d/e; 10a-R;9d-W;L16 10a-W	review	10d structural exercise Laugh 17 (shuo)	Unit 10d Prac READER Unit 10a-W
T 4/23	10d structure Intro 10b-R Laugh 17 (sh) Laugh 18 (t/n)	review	10a-R vocabulary Laugh 17 (xiang/xie) Laugh 18 (shuo)	Unit 10d Unit 10b-R READER
W 4/24	Prac 10b-R Intro 10b-W Laugh 18 (sh) Laugh 17 (overview)	review	10e structural exercise 10b-W vocabulary Laugh 18 (xiang/xie)	Unit 10e Unit 10b-R Unit 10b-W READER
Th 4/25 Intro 10c-R	10e structure Prac 10b-W Laugh 18 (overview)		10c-R vocabulary Unit 10c-R	Unit 10e Unit 10b-W READER
F 4/26	Use Unit 6a Prac 10c-R Laugh 19 (t/n)		Laugh 18 (shuo)	Unit 10c-R READER
M 4/29	TEST:10b/c-R;10a/b-W; L17/18 Intro 10d-R		10d-R vocabulary	Unit 10d-R
T 4/30	Prac 10d-R Intro 10c-W Laugh 19 (sh)		10c-W vocabulary Laugh 19 (xiang/xie)	Unit 10d-R Unit 10c-W READER
W 5/1	Prac 10c-W Laugh 20 (t/n)		Laugh 20 (shuo)	Unit 10c-W READER
Th 5/2	Intro 10e-R Divergent writing Laugh 20 (sh)		10e-R vocabulary Laugh 20 (xiang/xie)	Unit 10e-R READER
F 5/3	Prac 10e-R Divergent writing Role-play			Unit 10e-R
M 5/6	Divergent writing Role-play Review READER			
T 5/7	Divergent writing Role-play Review READER			
W 5/8	Review & summation			

5. Lesson planning

The syllabus provides a rough guide for planning at the semester level. Day by day, the teacher will need to plan in much greater detail, and to make preparations in support of the next day's activities. At the end of each class, the teacher might also assess what was accomplished, whether the objectives of the class were met, and make adjustments as necessary in planning the next day's class. I have found it useful to use a form like the one following, to serve as a planning guide for an upcoming class as well as a record of classes just completed.

Day #: _____ *Date:* _____

Activity planned	Materials needed	Done?	Comments

Following are examples of completed forms, following three days of actual classes.

Day #: 14   **Date:** 9/17 - Monday

Activity planned	Materials needed	Done?	Comments
Unit 2d - "use"	hand back personal sheet	✓	
✓ 20 questions	–	✓	good
✓ mingling act.	"little black notebook"	—	—
2a intro reading	—	✓	—
Introduce 2e	photograph	✓	need reinforcement

Day #: 15   **Date:** 9/18 – Tuesday

Activity planned	Materials needed	Done?	Comments
Structure notes p. 28	—	✓	—
Unit 1 writing	flashcards	✓	do in teams next time
2d oral practice	"little black notebook"	✓	give clearer instructions @ beginning
2e drill	table on overhead	✓	good!
2a reading	—	✓	o.k.

Day #: 16   **Date:** 9/19 – Wednesday

Activity planned	Materials needed	Done?	Comments
2d dialogue prac.	—	✓	—
2e line up by -height	—	✓	
-weight	—	✓	} great!
-birthday	—	✓	
1 writing prac.	namecards	✓	—

I hope you will find the suggestions in this volume useful. Often, it helps to be able to interact with and to observe and be observed by other teachers in other classes (sometimes even if they do not teach the same language as you). There are many, many factors that contribute to effective teaching and learning; these factors cannot be described adequately in a manual such as this. Observing others teach, having others critique your teaching, even learning a language you do not know from a teacher you believe to be effective: all these are useful and even indispensable for your own (unending) improvement as a teacher. Assuming the role of the student in a colleague's class can remind you of things you have forgotten, of what it is like to be a foreign language learner. If the colleague is at the same time trying to do the things you are attempting, for instance trying out activities like the ones described in this manual, you will have the added benefit of viewing such a curriculum from the vantage point of a student, and come to realize the some of the needs of a student.

Finally, if you have never worked with a "performance-based curriculum" before, as <u>Communicating in Chinese</u> aims to be, I urge you to take one or more workshops of the type offered by ACTFL. Even if they do not target Chinese language teaching, the principles described are the same, and can with some adaptation be applied to Chinese language classes. The type of teaching and learning this book facilitates involves some fundamental shifts in perspective from audio-lingual and grammar-translation syllabi. The more familiar you are with the basic concepts of communicative, interactive, task-based teaching and learning, the more successful you will be in implementing <u>Communicating in Chinese</u>.

If you have any suggestions, questions, or concerns, please write me at the Center for Chinese Studies, Moore Hall 416, University of Hawaii at Manoa, Honolulu, HI 96822; (808) 956-2692; FAX (808) 956-2682; e-mail:cyndy@uhunix.uhcc.hawaii.edu. Your comments are always welcome.

Introducing the Chinese sound system

Following the principle of presenting only so much information at a time as students can comfortably process, it is reasonable NOT to take the students through the entire *pinyin* syllabary in several intensive sittings at the very beginning of the semester. Rather, suggestions follow on how to familiarize students with the sounds of Chinese, using *Hanyu pinyin* as a guide, very gradually over an extended period of time (consistently throughout the first semester, sporadically thereafter for several years). A basic premise for these exercises is that, where possible, sounds should be affiliated with meaning. In any case, one shouldn't subject students to extended phonetic drills (that continue for longer than, say, fifteen minutes), without allowing them some glimpse of the meaning behind sounds. The activities below are listed approximately in the order I propose that you carry them out, not in an unbroken sequence from beginning to end, but interspersed with other activities from the body of the curriculum. Unit 1, for instance, should begin shortly after step 2 below. The remaining activities are best used at intervals, interspersed throughout the course of instruction, although #3-6 will probably be unnecessary beyond the first semester.

1. Introduce the numbers 1-10.

Numbers are such a familiar, essential concept, and so simple to learn in Chinese, that they form the easiest and most useful introduction to the sounds of Chinese.

•Teach the numbers 1-10 using the fingers of your two hands as a visual. Encourage the students to listen, and to react to each number as you say it by holding up the appropriate number of fingers. If they choose to repeat after you (in chorus), this should be allowed but not made mandatory; in any case, DO RESIST the urge (born of habit) to go around the room and call on individual students to say a number after you've "drilled" it a few times. At this point, your goal is to allow the students to hear some meaningful sounds of this foreign language, to begin to familiarize them with its sound system, and only peripherally to learn how to count. It is too early to call on individuals to "check pronunciation." You will be able to check individual pronunciation later, say during paired practice, when the student is not in the spotlight, so to speak, and has had many opportunities to test his own pronunciation privately.

After many (10-15) rounds of the "finger-play" listening comprehension drills (vary your routine after the first few by counting backwards from 10-1, by counting only even numbers, by counting only odd numbers, and finally by stating numbers at random), some students many be anxious to "take the stage" and try out their pronunciation publically, in which case you may wish to ask for volunteers to produce the numbers.

•To have the students begin to produce the numbers, write an Arabic numeral (1-10) on each of 10 cards, and repeat so that you will have enough cards to hand one to each student in the class. Distribute the cards IN RANDOM ORDER. Ask the students to take a moment to make sure they know how to say the number on the card they are holding. Then tell them that you will count together from 1-10 to a rhythm (clapped, slow at first and faster with each successive round). Each student is to hold up her card and call out the number on it at the appropriate moment in the sequence. After two or more rounds, have the students exchange cards with a classmate and repeat the process. Repeat until each student has had the opportunity to say several numbers. Vary the routine by counting backwards, even numbers only, etc.

•Break the students down into pairs. Give each pair one suite from a pack of cards, with the picture cards removed (see Card Drills in the Introduction). Have them check each other's production of numbers from 1-10. Move around the class and check pronunciation while this is happening.

2.   Introduce tones oral/aurally through number-mantras

Hum the first tone over and over again. Encourage the class to hum with you. Switch to singing la, la, la, la in first tone; encourage the class to sing with you. Then write the arabic numerals 1-3-7-8 on the board, and chant "yī, sān, qī, bā"; have the class chant with you. Repeat for as long as the class can stand to.

Next, hum several repetitions of the second tone. Encourage the class to hum with you. Switch to saying "yes? yes? yes? yes?" in the equivalent of a second tone. Have the class join in. Then write the number 10 on the board, and chant "shí, shí, shí, shí"; have the class chant with you. After a while, break the class into two groups, one chanting "yī, sān, qī, bā" and the other "harmonizing" with "shí, shí, shí, shí". After a minute or two, have the groups trade roles and repeat the assignment.

Hum several repetitions of the third tone. Encourage the class to hum with you. Switch to saying "well..., well..., well..., well..., " in the equivalent of a half-third tone (low, with no rise). Have the class join in. Then write the numbers 5 and 9 on the board, and chant "wǔ, jiǔ, wǔ, jiǔ" in half-third only (don't include the tone sandhi on wǔ) ; have the class chant with you. After a while, break the class into three groups, assign each a number-mantra, and proceed as before.

Finally, hum repetitions of the fourth tone. Encourage the class to hum with you. Switch to saying "yes! yes! yes! yes!" in the equivalent of a fourth tone. Have the class join in. Write the numbers 2-4-6...2 on the board and chant "èr, sì, liù...èr!"; have the class chant with you. Break the class into four groups, assign each a number-mantra, and proceed as before.

3.   Introduce the four tones and the numbers in *pinyin*.

An effective way to introduce *pinyin* is to let the students guess how to represent the numbers in *pinyin*. (If there is someone in the class who already knows *pinyin*, ask them to please not participate in this exercise.)

On the blackboard, draw four large tone marks and number them 1-4. Hum the four tones to demonstrate how they sound. Say the number yī, and have the students guess which tone it is, by holding up between one and four fingers (the correct answer is one finger). Repeat for the remaining numbers up to ten.

Next, ask the students to guess how to spell yī using the roman alphabet. They will guess combinations such as "ee," "i," "ii" etc. Write all their guesses on the blackboard, and draw symbols to show when they are getting "warmer" and "colder." If you are lucky, someone will finally guess "yi." If not, write it for them when they run out of guesses. BE ENCOURAGING AT ALL TIMES. Continue through the rest of the numbers 1-10, and prepare to spend extra time on the numbers 4, 6, 7, and 10.

4.   Work on the numbers 11-999.

Once the students are comfortable with 1-10, they will more or less be able to figure out 11-99 on their own, with minimal help from you. Flash 11 fingers (two motions: first all ten fingers, then one finger) and say "shíyī." Encourage them to repeat it. Then flash 12 fingers and wait for a response. When you get it, continue until 19. Try flashing 20 (two motions: all ten fingers palm out, then all ten fingers with the palms facing you), and if no-one guesses "èrshí," you will have to tell them. Continue until, say, 50, and then in increments (55, 60, 65, 70..) until 95. You will have to tell them "yìbǎi." After that, you may wish to continue until 999. A grade school number chart or some counting beads would be useful as a visual aid. If you wish, continue on and teach them "yíwàn."

5.   Introduce word initials.

Take the Word Initial sheet directly following this section. Make photocopies so that each student can have one sheet, then cut apart into flashcards and store each set in an envelope. You may wish to laminate the cards, punch a hole in the corner of each, secure each set with a key-ring through the holes, and keep the sets permanently for distribution to and recollection from the students.

Distribute one set of cards to each student. Take one set yourself. Have the students lay the cards out on the table before them. Do the same yourself. Call out a syllable, and have the students pick up the corresponding card and hold it up. Repeat until most of the students are getting most of the cues right most of the time (no longer than 10 minutes).

6.   Introduce word finals.

Repeat the process described for word initials with the Word Final cue cards. Since there are many more finals than initials, work on a portion of the whole at a time.

7.   Work with parts of the syllabary.

•Write out selected syllables from the syllabary in large letters on a 5"x8" card.

•Hold up two cards at a time. Say the word on one of those two cards. Have the students point to the appropriate card. Replace that card with another and repeat. Continue the activity for 5-10 minutes.

•Distribute 1 card to each student. When you call out a word, the student holding the appropriate card is to raise it up. Continue until all the words have been called. Have the students exchange cards and repeat. Continue this activity for 5-10 minutes.

•Have your students form groups of 3-4, and sit in their groups along the outer perimeter of the classroom. Make a large tic-tac-toe grid in the center of the floor using masking tape. Number each space from 1-9 by writing with chalk or by pasting down a numbered card with masking tape. Lay one syllabary card in each square of the grid. A spokesperson from each group in turn picks a word to pronounce (by announcing its number), and then pronounces it. If she is right, repeat the pronunciation, remove the card (place it in a "DONE" stack), and award the group a point. If she is wrong, the turn passes to another group. Do NOT provide the correct pronunciation. When all the cards in the grid have been removed, replace them with fresh ones and begin again. If a few cards remain in the grid and all the groups have failed to pronounce them correctly, call "Time out," pronounce the words correctly once or twice, remove the cards and shuffle them into the "NOT YET DONE" stack and begin again with fresh cards. Continue for 10-15 minutes. Members of the group with the highest number of points at the end of the game wins.

8. Teach some basic classroom commands.

•Using a combination of Total Physical Response and pantomime, teach the class expressions such as the following. (Don't feel compelled to teach all of them!)

√Qing zhan qilai. (Stand up.)
√Qing zuo xia. (Sit down.)
√Qing zhuyi ting. (Cup hand behind ear.)
√Qing zhuyi kan. (Shade eyes.)
√Qing ba dongxi fang hao. (Arm sweeps top of desk.)
√Qing ni shuo. (Hand makes the motion of a duck's beak quacking in front of the
    mouth, using the four fingers and opposing thumb.)
√Qing ni zai shuo yici. (Hand circles to indicate repeat, then makes quacking motion.)
√Qing ni da sheng yidiar shuo. (Use two hands to quack, with fingers widespread.)
√Qing ni xiao sheng yidiar shuo. (Use forefinger and thumb only to quack.)

√*Qing bie shuohua.* (Warning finger in front of lips.)
√*Qing zhao yige huoban.* (Link arms with someone else in class.)

•Divide the students into pairs. Hand out scratch paper and two large sheets of paper (11.5" x 14", if available; other wise 8.5" x 11" would suffice) and a marking pen to each pair. Assign one classroom expression to each pair, have them render it into *pinyin* and then print the *pinyin* carefully on scratch paper. Next, have two pairs get together to edit each other's work, then copy the edited work carefully, in large visible script using the marking pen, onto one of the large pieces of paper. Edit these together as a class. Finally, have each pair copy the corrected versions onto their second sheet of paper, and tape these to the wall.

9. Teach Tang poetry.

These provide some welcome cultural interludes, but don't do too many or the students may feel overwhelmed! One or two per semester should more than suffice, although you may want to use several for cursory transcription exercises as described below. They are cultural artifacts that native speakers memorize and quote from to lend color and depth to daily conversations. They are also linguistic artifacts in the native-speaking environment that are always carefully enunciated, with special attention paid to tones and tone-patterns, and for this reason they serve as admirable targets for pronunciation practice. The fact that most are very beautiful to hear is an added benefit.

•Say a poem slowly and clearly, and have the students draw its tone patterns (tones only, no initials or finals) on a piece of paper. Check together.

•Photocopy the "Step 2" handout (using Li Bo's <u>Ye Si</u>; if you prefer, select another poem and adapt it accordingly) and distribute to each student. Repeat the poem, and have the students fill in the blanks. Check together.

•Photocopy the "Step 3" handout below (using Li Bo's <u>Ye Si</u>; if you prefer, select another poem and adapt it accordingly) and distribute to each student. Repeat the poem, and have the students fill in the blanks. Check together.

•Have the students transcribe the poem in *pinyin* on a blank sheet of paper as you recite it to them. Check together.

•Have the students put away the poem and take out a sheet of blank paper. Hand the poem (in *pinyin*) to a volunteer, and have him dictate one line while the others (including you) write the tones as you hear them. Check together. Repeat with other volunteers for other lines.

•You may want to have the students memorize one poem of their choice, and try to recite it for you totally accurately sometime during the course of the semester.

Initials

b-	p-	m-	f-
d-	t-	n-	l-
g-	k-	h-	
z-	c-	s-	
j-	q-	x-	
zh-	ch-	sh-	r-
y-	w-		

Finals

-ai	-ao	-an	-ang
-ei	-en	-eng	-ia
-ie	-iu	-in	-ing
-iao	-ian	-iang	-iong
-ou	-ong	-ua	-ui
-üe	-(ü)n	-(ü)an	
-uo	-un	-uai	-uan
-uang			

Step Two handout

Write in the word initials as you hear them.

Ye Si by Li Bo

____uáng ____ián ____íng ____uè ____uāng

____í ____ì ____ì ____àng ____uāng

____ǔ ____óu ____àng ____íng ____uè

____ī ____óu ____ī ____ù ____iāng

- -

Step Three handout

Write in the word finals as you hear them.

Ye Si by Li Bo

ch____ q ____ m ____ y____ g____

y____ sh____ d____ sh____ sh____

j____ t____ w____ m____ y____

d____ t____ s____ g____ x____

Yè Sī by Li Bo

床前明月光，

chuáng qián míng yuè guāng

bed - in front - bright - moon - light

Bright moonlight falls in front of my bed;

疑是地上霜，

yí shì dì shàng shuāng

to suspect - to be - ground - on top - frost

I take it for frost on the ground.

舉頭望明月，

jǔ tóu wàng míng yuè

to raise - head - to gaze at - bright - moon

Lifting my head, I gaze at the moon;

低頭思故鄉。

dī tóu sī gù xiāng

lower - head - to think of - old - village

dropping my head, I think of my home.

Unit 1

Materials required

• Two hand puppets of any type. Chinese puppets would be nice, but picture cutouts, photographs, toys etc. would serve as well.

• Poker chips in white and red, so that half the class can have one of each; a paper sack.

Introduction

• Walk around the room shaking hands with each student, saying Ni hao. (The students may either respond or not, depending on how confident they feel.)

• Using two hand puppets, simulate a dialogue between two people. Have them nod to each other as they exchange greetings. Include variations of Ni hao.

• Go around the room again to each student, this time nodding Ni hao, and adding Zai jian accompanied by a wave goodbye (hold your right hand up, palm forward, and wave from side to side) before you move on.

• Wave at random to members of the class, saying variations of Zai jian.

• Using the puppets, introduce Qing... and Xiexie. (Pantomime offering and receiving something, for example.) Say Xiexie repeatedly and accompany it with the Chinese gesture for "thank you" (make your left hand into a fist, clasp your right hand over it, and shake both hands lightly up and down with a slight bow or nod). Repeat Qing with an appropriate motion of offering (forward motion of the hand with palm up).

• Pantomime a context to introduce Duibuqi (pretend to step on a student's foot, or knock an item off his or her desk, for example). Say Duibuqi over and over again, accompanied by some sort of a gesture to indicate regret (place one hand over the mouth, or clasp both temples, for example).

• Use the hand puppets to simulate dialogues in which all variations of Xiexie and Duibuqi are introduced.

Comprehension Drills

• Have the students make gestures as you repeat the items in the lesson: nod for Ni hao, wave for Zai jian, palm up/forward motion of the hand for Qing, clasped hands for Xiexie, and one hand on the mouth for Duibuqi, for example. Include all variations of each expression.

Oral Practice

• To practice greetings and goodbyes, have the students form Inner/Outer circles and practice greeting and taking leave from successive classmates. Check them for proper posture and body language (nodding is appropriate for both hello and goodbye).

• To practice expressions of gratitude and regret, place the red and white poker chips in the sack. Take out one of each color, and explain to the students the cultural meaning of the colors red and white (see the Cultural notes to Unit 6a). Return the chips to the bag. Go around the room to each student in turn; invite him/her (say <u>Qing..</u>) to feel blindly for a chip and take it out. If it is red, he has received a symbol of happiness from you, and should say <u>Xiexie</u> to you (respond with <u>Buxie</u> or an equivalent). If it is white, he has received a symbol of sorrow. You should apologize, and the student should respond with <u>Meiyou guanxi</u>.

• Have the students listen to the audiotape and complete the Dialog Practice exercise for homework. Check in class.

• Divide the class into pairs to rehearse "A Brief Encounter." Have two or three pairs perform for the class, by reading aloud if necessary, or from memory. The students need not reproduce the language in the conversation exactly—it suffices to convey the appropriate meaning in acceptable language,

Controlled use

• Have the students form Inner/outer circles. Students in the Outer circle receive one red chip and one white chip each, and distribute them between their two closed fists. Their partners in the Inner circle first greet them, then select one of the two fists, and depending upon whether the red or the white chip is revealed, either say "thank you" or receive an apology. The two students say goodbye before the circle rotates.

Unit 2a

Materials required

• Blank 5" X 8" index cards (one each for teacher and students); magic markers.

• Unit pictures.

Introduction

• Introduce wo/ni/ta/women/nimen/tamen by using appropriate hand gestures (for example: thumb at chest to indicate wo, or in the Chinese style, forefinger touching the tip of the nose; forefinger forward to indicate ni, thumb jerked to one side to indicate ta, waggle thumb at chest to indicate women, waggle forefinger to indicate nimen, waggle open palm to one side to indicate tamen).

• Make (or have your students make) name cards as follows. Fold an index card in half lengthwise. With the fold on top, write the name in English on one outer surface of the folded card, and (if available) in Chinese (pinyin) on the other. Make sure that you and each student has a name card. Distribute the cards and have the students place them on their desks, English forward to begin with, so that all cards are legible to everyone. (At some point you may wish to reverse the cards to introduce the students to each other by their Chinese names, if these are available.) Introduce the operations involved in naming and introductions by beginning with your own name as an example, and then proceeding around the room. (Wo xing Doe. Ni xing Smith. Ni xing Wang. Ni xing Nakayama.etc.) Begin with xing; then proceed to jiao (Wo jiao John. Ni jiao Debbie); do shi last (Wo shi John Doe. Ni shi Debbie Smith. etc.) You may want to indicate that jiao and shi are sometimes interchangeable.

• Introduce dui and budui by first demonstrating and then asking "loaded questions," such as Wo xing Smith, duibudui? Budui, wo xing Doe. Ta ne? Ta xing Wang ma? Dui, ta xing Wang. Ni xing Rodriguez, duibudui? Dui...)

• Introduce the surnames Zhang/Wang/Li/Chen/Ma using the unit pictures.

Comprehension Drills

• With the name cards in place, ask questions such as Shei xing Rodriguez? Shei jiao Mary? Shei shi Richard Wang? Shei de mingzi jiao Hideko? etc. one at a time, and have the students point out their classmates as you name them.

• Repeat with the name cards removed.

• Distribute the name cards at random to the students, and have them role-play each other. Mary Smith, for example, may be holding Hideko Yamauchi's card, and would now answer for him. Make statements such as Ni xing Wang, Ni de mingzi jiao Mary, Ni shi Ari Kalinowski, to identify each student in the class (more than once each, by last name, by first name, by full name). As each name is called out, the role-playing student raises his/her hand. The cards can be collected, shuffled, and redistributed again, to provide further drilling. If desired (and if your students are able), conduct the above exercises using the students' Chinese names.

• Distribute the pictures at random, one to each student. Say the surnames <u>Zhang/Wang/ Li/Chen/Ma</u> one at a time <u>(Shei xing Zhang?)</u>, and have the students holding the appropriate portraits raise them.

Oral Practice

• Seat the students in one large circle; have them take out a pen or pencil and a sheet of paper. By Visiting, have every student briefly interview each of his/her classmates, to find out (or confirm) his/her real name. <u>(Ni shi shei? Ni xing shenme? Ni shi Mary Smith ma?</u> etc. Make sure they use the polite form <u>nin</u> when they speak to you.) The students write down what they learn as they go around, so that by the time they return to their seats, they have developed a personal class roster.

• Have the students listen to the audiotape and complete the Dialog Practice exercise for homework. Check in class.

• Divide the class into groups of 3 to rehearse "Recognition." Have 2-3 groups perform.

• Brainstorm for variations on the sample statements and questions provided. List these on an overhead transparency, and then photocopy for distribution to the students as additional (personalized) input.

Controlled use

• Teacher and student each secretly pick one well-known person they will role-play. Repeat the Visiting activity used above to find out which person everyone in the class is playing. Students write each role-play name next to the real name on their rosters. You may wish to join in this activity, to develop a master list of your own. Finally, check the rosters together.

Unit 2b

Materials required

•A slide or an enlarged photograph of any family meaningful to the students (including your own), depicting a wife, husband, one grown daughter, and others as available.

•Students' name cards used in Unit 2a.

•Blank 3" X 5" index cards; magic marker; tape.

Introduction

•Display the family photograph, state the last name of its members (Tamen xing Smith..), and then introduce each in turn (Zhei shi Smith Xiansheng; Zhei shi Smith Taitai; Zhei shi Smith Xiaojie). Point to both the wife and the daughter and introduce nüshi (Tamen dou shi Smith nüshi).

•Using Guessing, introduce each person in the picture-cards provided.

Comprehension Drills

•Students use their individual sets of the portraits, and hold up the appropriate one in response to prompts such as the following.

> Zhei wei shi Zhang Xiansheng.
> Nei wei shi Lao Li.
> Lao Li hen hao.
> Xiao Ma ye hen hao.
> Zhang nüshi, Li Xiaojie ye dou hen hao.
> Nei wei shi Li Tongzhi.
> Li Tongzhi de mingzi jiao Datong.

Oral Practice

•Write each of the terms of address (Xiansheng, Taitai, etc.) on one or more index cards, so that there is one card for each student in the class. Distribute the cards at random, disregarding gender (a male student may receive a Taitai card). Distribute the name cards, also at random. Students tape the title cards to their chests, and place the name cards on their desks. Go around the room once with the students taking turns introducing their neighbor to the class. Be sure to use the role-play names and titles assigned to each (Ta shi Smith/Simisi Xiangsheng; Ta shi Lao Wang; Ta shi xiao meimei; etc.). Using Visiting, students then take turns greeting and being greeted by each of their classmates. (Smith/Simisi Tongzhi, ni hao; O, Lao Wang, ni hao; xiao meimei, ni hao, etc.) Students should shake hands or nod to each other during the exchanges.

•Have the students listen to the audiotape and complete the Dialog Practice exercise for homework. Check in class.

•Divide the class into groups of 4 to rehearse "The Following Day." Have 2-3 groups perform.

•Brainstorm for variations of the sample statements and questions provided. List these on an overhead transparency, and then photocopy for distribution to the students as additional (personalized) input.

Controlled use

•Each student brings in a magazine or newspaper photograph of a person, old or young, male or female, well-known or not, to role-play during this activity. The student should know the identity of the person in his or her own photograph; the photograph is then taped to the student's chest. Using Visiting, the students go around the room and greet each classmate's persona appropriately. If Student A knows the identity of Student B's persona (say, Marilyn Monroe), Student A need simply to greet Student B appropriately: Monroe Xiaojie/ Monroe Nüshi, ni hao. Supposing however, that Student B does not recognize Student A's persona. Student B would first need to ask, Duibuqi, qingwen gui xing?/ Duibuqi, ni jiao shenme mingzi? and understand the answer, before he or she could proceed with O, Montana Xiansheng, ni hao.

•After all students have gone around once, identify each persona in the room (Nin gui xing? Wo xing Monroe; Ni shi shei? Wo shi Joe Montana; Ni jiao shenme mingzi? Wo jiao Kermit). Follow each identification with an appropriate greeting by the class as a group (to Kermit: Xiao pengyou, ni hao)

Unit 2c

Materials required

•Reprints of the master provided in this unit.

•Unit pictures.

Introduction

•Use Pantomime to introduce the descriptive terms in this lesson.

Comprehension Drills

•Use Pantomime and/or Picture-card drills, in which the students respond to cues such as the following.

> *Ta hen bai.*
> *Ni juede wo haokan ma?*
> *Ni you ai, you pang. Ni you gao, you shou.*
> *Lao Li hen chou.*
> *Zheiwei xiao meimei hen piaoliang.*

Oral Practice

•Distribute one copy of "Is Mr. Wang fat?" to each student. Have them form pairs, and complete the task given.

•Have the students listen to the audiotape and complete the Dialog Practice exercise for homework. Check in class.

•Divide the class into groups of 3 to rehearse "Among Friends." Have 2-3 groups perform for the class.

•Brainstorm for variations of the sample statements and questions provided. List these on an overhead transparency, and then photocopy for distribution to the students as additional (personalized) input.

Controlled use

•Divide the class into two to four teams, depending on the size of your class. Have each team secretly name one teacher or administrator in your school, who will likely be known to everyone in the class. The teams then take turns playing Twenty Questions to guess the identities of the persons selected. Questions asked may include <u>Ta gao ma? Pang ma? Shi Xiansheng ma? Shi Taitai ma?</u> etc.

Unit 2c: "Is Mr. Wáng fat?"

Mark with * any ONE selection from each column below.

Mark with + any ONE selection from each column below.

Mark with Δ any ONE selection from each column below.

Name	Title	Attribute
Zhāng	Xiānsheng	gāo
Wáng	Tàitai	ǎi
Lǐ	Xiáojiě	pàng
Chén	Nǚshì	shòu
Mǎ	Lǎo	hēi
	Xiǎo	bái
		zhuàng
		ruò
		hǎokàn
		nánkàn

You have now created three people, each with a title, a last name, and a descriptive attribute. Your partner has done the same. Your goal is to find out details about each of your partner's three people, and your partner will do the same for you. To achieve this goal, you will need to ask and answer questions. Begin with the person marked with *. Both you and your partner will pretend to be the person you each have created, and take turns interrogating each other along the lines of the model provided below. Note that your questions must elicit yes/no answers.

Nǐ xìng Zhāng ma?	Wǒ xìng Zhāng. / Wǒ bú xìng Zhāng.
Nǐ xìng Lǐ ma?	Wǒ xìng Lǐ. / Wǒ bú xìng Lǐ.
Nǐ shì Zhāng Xiānsheng ma?	Shì. / Bú shì.
Nǐ shì Láo Lǐ ma?	Shì. / Bú shì.
Nǐ gāo bù gāo?	Wó hěn gāo. / Wǒ bù gāo.

Based on the responses your partner gives you, complete the sentences outlined below.

(*) _____ .
    (name & title)   *(attribute)*

(+)_____ .
    (name & title)   *(attribute)*

(Δ)_____ .
    (name & title)   *(attribute)*

Check your work by reading your sentences aloud to your partner, who will compare them against his or her originals.

Unit 2d

Materials required
• Reprints of the masters provided. Wide tipped, dark pens; tape.

Introduction
• Distribute one copy each of "Wo" to the students. Have them fill out the form with a wide-tipped pen, and tape it to their chest. Ask a volunteer to come to the front of the class, and describe that person based on the information on his or her form. (Zhei shi Zhang Meiying. Ta ershi sui le. Ta nian san nianji. Ta zhu Oak jie, yibaqijiu hao, C-san shi. Ta de dianhua haoma shi wu-san-er, ba-ba-jiu-qi.) Repeat with four or five more volunteers, as necessary. Alternatively, go around the room describing one characteristic at a time (Ni shiqi suile; ni shiba suile; ni ershi sui le etc.). When done, have the students take the forms off, write their names in pencil on the reverse side, and turn them in to you. After class, make a copy of each of their forms, so that you will have a complete set.

Comprehension Drills
• Return the original "Wo" forms to the respective students. Have them sit in a circle, with the forms taped to their chests. Based on information taken from your complete set of forms, call out cues as in the following models.

> Wo de dianhua haoma shi 737-8097.
> Wo shiliu sui le.
> Wo zhu zai Niuyue shi.
> Wo zhu 17 jie, 209 hao. etc.

Students to whom the cues pertain should signal by raising their hands. Continue until all information in your set has been stated at least once. When the drill is over, collect the students' "Wo" forms from them.

Oral Practice
• Take the original set of "Wo" forms, remove one at random, and place it inside a folder. Give the folder to a student volunteer, and have the rest of the class determine whose form is in the folder by playing Twenty Questions. Repeat as appropriate.

• Have the students listen to the audiotape and complete the Dialog Practice exercise for homework. Check in class.

• Divide the class into pairs to rehearse "More Information." Have 2-3 groups perform for the class.

• Brainstorm for variations of the sample statements and questions provided. List these on an overhead transparency, and then photocopy for distribution to the students as additional (personalized) input.

Controlled use
• Distribute one copy each of "The little black book" to the students, and have them complete the task assigned by Mingling.

Unit 2d: "Wǒ"

Please fill in the blanks below as indicated, writing in LARGE, CLEAR print.

Niánlíng: _____

(write your age)

Niánjí: _____

(write your grade or class level)

Dìzhǐ:

_____ shì

(write the city you live in)

_____ jiē

(write the street on which you live)

_____ hào

(write the number of your house or building)

_____ shì

(write your apartment number)

Diànhuà hàomǎ:

_____

(write your telephone number)

Unit 2d: The little black notebook

Obtain the following information from as many of your classmates as you can, in the time allotted.

Name	Age	Address	Telephone #

Unit 2e

Materials required

•Photographs of three–four prominent sports figures, with information on their height, weight, and birthday.

•Reprints of the masters provided.

Introduction

Some students, particularly adolescents, are hesitant about revealing their height and weight. It would probably be best to let your students volunteer information, if they wish to, in this lesson, and not insist that any student divulge facts he or she would rather keep private.

•Tape the photograph of one of the sports figures to the blackboard. Write personal specifics for that person on the blackboard in English (MICHAEL JORDAN. Height: 6' 6"; Weight: 195 lbs; Birthday: February 17, 1963.) Now describe that person in Chinese, pointing to the English equivalents as you say the Chinese, to help your students understand what you are saying. Repeat, restate, be redundant.

•Repeat this process for the remaining sports figures, encouraging your students to make guesses and contribute information that they have.

•Ask for a volunteer to state his/her own specifications. Draw (or have a student draw) a cariacature of the volunteer on the blackboard to parallel the photographs taped there; then guess (and encourage the class to guess) the height, weight, and birthday of the student. Repeat this process as necessary.

Comprehension Drills

•Have your students contribute information about the height, weight, and birthday of one person each—either him/herself, or else someone whose specifications are public information. Collect this information from them. Make a copy of "Who's who", and on this copy, write the name only of ten of the individuals identified by your students in the spaces provided. Leave the rest of the blanks unfilled. Make copies of this master for the entire class. After the copies have been made, fill in the rest of the blank spaces on your master copy, using the information you have collected. Make an overhead transparency of this filled-in master copy.

Distribute the student version of "Who's who". Read out a name, and then one bit of information for that person; have your students fill in the appropriate blank based on what you have read. Continue at random, skipping from detail to detail, until all the information for each person on your list has been stated at least once. Check your students' comprehension by using the overhead.

Oral Practice

•Make a copy of "Who's who." Using the information previously gathered by your students, write in ten names on the copy, preferably of people who were not discussed in the Drilling session. Repeat the activity used for Drilling, except that this time the students have to ask for specific pieces of information. (Reggie Jackson duo gao? Ta you duo zhong? Ta de shengri shi jiyue jihao?)

•Have the students listen to the audiotape and complete the Dialog Practice exercise for homework. Check in class.

•Divide the class into pairs to rehearse "Further Information." Have 2-3 groups perform.

•Brainstorm for variations of the sample statements and questions provided.

Controlled use

Distribute "Our class" to the students, one copy each. Using Inner/Outer circles, have them interview each other for height, weight, and birthday. Each student should divulge at least one piece of information. For anything the student chooses not to share, he/she may simply state Wo bu gaosu ni. Check the results on an overhead transparency.

60

Unit 2e: Who's who

Fill in the blanks below, based on information provided.

Name	Height	Weight	Birthday
1.			
2.			
3.			
4.			
5.			
6.			
7.			
8.			
9.			
10.			

Unit 2e: Our Class

Interview your classmates to find out the following pieces of information. If they refuse to tell you something, write "wx" (<u>wèixiáng</u>="unknown") in the space. Do collect at least one piece of information from each person.

	Name	Height	Weight	Birthday
1.				
2.				
3.				
4.				
5.				
6.				
7.				
8.				
9.				
10.				
11.				
12.				
13.				
14.				
15.				
16.				
17.				
18.				
19.				
20.				

Unit 2f

Materials required

• Copies of the Class roster, one per student.

• Reprints of the masters provided.

• Unit pictures.

Introduction

• Use Pantomime to introduce the vocabulary of this lesson.

Comprehension Drills

• Use Picture-card drills.

Oral Practice

• Photocopy one or more sets of the picture cards so that each student will have one card for one individual occupation. Distribute them at random; the card that the student gets will be the occupation he/she will role-play for this activity. Pass out one copy of the roster to each student. Using Mingling or Inner/outer circles, have the students ask each other yes/no questions to find out which occupations they are role-playing, and write in the information on their rosters. Go over the information together when finished.

• Have the students listen to the audiotape and complete the Dialog Practice exercise for homework. Check in class.

• Divide the class into pairs to rehearse "Aspirations." Have 2-3 groups perform for the class.

• Brainstorm for variations of the sample statements and questions provided.

Controlled use

• Ask your students to form pairs. Distribute one set each of the A and B versions of "What's the scoop?" to each pair, and have them complete the task assigned.

2f: What's the scoop? (A)

Pretend you and your partner are census takers. You have interviewed the Zhao family and filled in forms 1-4. Your partner has interviewed the Jiang family and filled in forms 5-8. You are now on the telephone to your partner; exchange information so that you each have a completed set of eight forms.

The Zhaos

1. Name: _Zhào Huá_

Age: _36_   Tel: _956 - 2682_

Address: _#2031   10th Ave._
Lake City

Occupation: _secretary_

2. Xìngmíng:. _Lǐ Jīngníng_

Niánlíng: _34_   Diànhuà: _732-2075_

Dìzhǐ: _#108   15th St._
Lake City

Zhíyè: _teacher_

3. Xìngmíng: _Zhào Zhēnyǎ_

Niánlíng: _15_   Diànhuà: _253-0600_

Dìzhǐ: _#449   17th. Ave._
Lake City

Zhíyè: _student_

4. Xìngmíng: _Zhào Zhèndōng_

Niánlíng: _8_   Diànhuà: _253-0600_

Dìzhǐ: _#449   17th Ave._
Lake City

Zhíyè: _student_

The Jiangs

5. Xìngmíng: _____

Niánlíng: _____ Diànhuà: _____

Dìzhǐ: _____
_____

Zhíyè: _____

6. Xìngmíng: _____

Niánlíng: _____ Diànhuà: _____

Dìzhǐ: _____
_____

Zhíyè: _____

7. Xìngmíng: _____

Niánlíng: _____ Diànhuà: _____

Dìzhǐ: _____
_____

Zhíyè: _____

8. Xìngmíng: _____

Niánlíng: _____ Diànhuà: _____

Dìzhǐ: _____
_____

Zhíyè: _____

2f: What's the scoop? (B)

Pretend you and your partner are census takers. You have interviewed the Jiang family and filled in forms 5-8. Your partner has interviewed the Zhao family and filled in forms 1-4. You are now on the telephone to your partner; exchange information so that you each have a completed set of eight forms.

The Zhaos

1. Name: _____

Age: _____ Tel: _____

Address: _____

_____

Occupation: _____

2. Xìngmíng: _____

Niánlíng: _____ Diànhuà: _____

Dìzhǐ: _____

Zhíyè: _____

3. Xìngmíng: _____

Niánlíng: _____ Diànhuà: _____

Dìzhǐ: _____

_____

Zhíyè: _____

4. Xìngmíng: _____

Niánlíng: _____ Diànhuà: _____

Dìzhǐ: _____

_____

Zhíyè: _____

The Jiangs

5. Xìngmíng: _Jiāng Xuéxián_

Niánlíng: _47_ Diànhuà: _250-2073_

Dìzhǐ: _1830 University Ave._
Jinyang City

Zhíyè: _secretary_

6. Xìngmíng: _Wáng Xiǎoqing_

Niánlíng: _48_ Diànhuà: _842-0075_

Dìzhǐ: _17 Jiangsu Rd._
Mashan City

Zhíyè: _attorney_

7. Xìngmíng: _Jiāng Tiānming_

Niánlíng: _24_ Diànhuà: _255-8216_

Dìzhǐ: _Gǔlóuxī Ave. #29_
Mashan City

Zhíyè: _attorney_

8. Xìngmíng: _Jiāng Zhàoming_

Niánlíng: _18_ Diànhuà: _572-8619_

Dìzhǐ: _Guānhǎi Ave. #43_
Jinyang City

Zhíyè: _waiter in restaurant_

Unit 2g

Materials required

• Map of the world—either a wall map or an overhead transparency.

• Reprints of the masters provided.

• Unit pictures.

Introduction

• Use the instructor's set of picture cards and Guessing to introduce the names of the countries and regions. Reinforce by pointing to places on the world map.

• Say random selections from the following list of greetings, one at a time. Pause after each expression and use Guessing: ask the students to guess which of two languages they have just heard (Hanguohua haishi Ribenhua?), while you hold up the picture cards of those two places. The students respond by pointing to one or the other.

*Ni hao *Chinese*	*Konnichiwa *Japanese*	*Anyong haseyo *Korean*
*Namaste *Hindi*	Hello *English*	Bonjour *French*
Guten Tag *German*	Que pasa *Spanish*	*Zdrastvuite *Russian*

*indicates romanization of native writing system

Comprehension Drills

• Use Picture-card drills. Besides the usual prompts, include questions such as "Guten Tag" shi Deguo hua haishi Faguohua?

• Students write the name of a foreign language they have studied on a blank index card, in LARGE, DARK PRINT, and tape these to their chests. (They may choose to pretend they know a foreign language they haven't actually studied.) Make statements such as "Ta hui shuo Indu hua," and have the students who have selected the language mentioned raise their cards.

Oral Practice

• Have students find out from each other what languages they speak. (Use fact or make-believe, depending on how foreign language-savvy your students are.) Use pair-work, Inner/Outer Circle, or Mingling format. You may wish to distribute a copy of the class roster to each student, to facilitate their gathering information from each of their classmates. Check their work on the blackboard or overhead projector.

•Have your students form pairs. Distribute "Where are you from?" and have the students complete the assignment.

•Have the students listen to the audiotape and complete the Dialog Practice exercise for homework. Check in class.

•Divide the class into groups of 4 to rehearse "On Foreign Languages." Have 2-3 groups perform for the class.

•Brainstorm for variations of the sample statements and questions provided.

Controlled use

•Ask your students to form pairs. Distribute a copy of "What's the scoop?" to each student, and have the students work in pairs to complete the task assigned.

Unit 2g: Where are you from?

Twelve people are named below, as well as twelve places of origin. At random, match the people with the places by writing the number of the place in the appropriate blank in column A; your partner will do the same.
MAKE SURE YOU USE EVERY COUNTRY ONCE.

Your task is to guess the numbers your partner has written; he/she will do the same for you. Do this by asking questions. The questions you may ask are written in italics at the bottom of the page; you may ask each question ONLY AS MANY TIMES AS THERE ARE CIRCLES FOLLOWING IT in the first column for you, and the second column for your partner.

You ask questions of your partner first. When you have asked all your questions, your turn is over; the number of correct guesses you have made in column B is your score. Your partner will now begin; keep track of his/her questions by marking the appropriate circles. The maximum score is 12; the person with the higher score wins.

		A	**B**
Zhāng Xiānsheng	1. Měiguó		
Wáng Nǔshì	2. Zhōngguó		
Lǐ Xiáojiě	3. Rìběn		
Lǎo Chén	4. Hánguó		
Tán Lǎoshī	5. Yìndù		
Lǎo Ōu	6. Dōngnányà		
Xiǎo Dèng	7. Zhōngdōng		
Zhōu Xiānsheng	8. Yīngguó		
Bái Xiáojiě	9. Fàguó		
Yú Tàitài	10. Déguó		
Fāng Yīshēng	11. Xībānyà		
Xiǎo Kuàng	12. Èguó		

Questions you may ask:

Check off one circle below each time you ask a particular question.
Check off one circle below each time your partner asks a question.

_____ shì něiguó rén?   O O O   O O O
(person)

_____ cóng nǎr lái de?   O O O   O O O
(person)

_____ jiā zài nǎr?   O O O   O O O
(person)

_____ shì _____ rén ma?   O O O O   O O O O
(person)　　(place)

                           O O O O   O O O O

*Score:*_____

2g: What's the scoop? (A)

Pretend you and your partner are census takers. You have interviewed the Zhang family and filled in forms 1-4. Your partner has interviewed the Fang family and filled in forms 5-8. You are now on the telephone to your partner; exchange information so that you each have a completed set of eight forms.

The Zhangs

1. Name: Zhāng Shūhuì
Age: 19   Tel: 250-1188
Address: 27 Báishíqiáo Rd.
Nationality: British
Occupation: police officer

2. Xìngmíng: Sòng Zhìguó
Niánlíng: 54 Diànhuà: 427-2464
Dìzhǐ: 28 Báishíqiáo Rd.
Guójí: German
Zhíyè: sales clerk

3. Xìngmíng: Zhāng Dàolín
Niánlíng: 31 Diànhuà: 831-4989
Dìzhǐ: 27 Báishíqiáo Rd.
Guójí: German
Zhíyè: doctor

4. Xìngmíng: Zhāng Jìngxióng
Niánlíng: 27 Diànhuà: 250-6421
Dìzhǐ: 503 Dōngfēng Rd.
Guójí: Spanish
Zhíyè: farmer

The Fangs

5. Xìngmíng: _____
Niánlíng: _____ Diànhuà: _____
Dìzhǐ: _____
Guójí: _____
Zhíyè: _____

6. Xìngmíng: _____
Niánlíng: _____ Diànhuà: _____
Dìzhǐ: _____
Guójí: _____
Zhíyè: _____

7. Xìngmíng: _____
Niánlíng: _____ Diànhuà: _____
Dìzhǐ: _____
Guójí: _____
Zhíyè: _____

8. Xìngmíng: _____
Niánlíng: _____ Diànhuà: _____
Dìzhǐ: _____
Guójí: _____
Zhíyè: _____

2g: What's the scoop? (B)

Pretend you and your partner are census takers. You have interviewed the Fang family and filled in forms 5-8 Your partner has interviewed the Zhang family and filled in forms 1-4. You are now on the telephone to your partner; exchange information so that you each have a completed set of eight forms.

The Zhangs

1. Name: _____

Age: _____ Tel: _____

Address: _____

Nationality: _____

Occupation: _____

2. Xìngmíng: _____

Niánlíng: _____ Diànhuà: _____

Dìzhǐ: _____

Guójí: _____

Zhíyè: _____

3. Xìngmíng: _____

Niánlíng: _____ Diànhuà: _____

Dìzhǐ: _____

Guójí: _____

Zhíyè: _____

4. Xìngmíng: _____

Niánlíng: _____ Diànhuà: _____

Dìzhǐ: _____

Guójí: _____

Zhíyè: _____

The Fangs

5. Xìngmíng: Fāng Dàyǒng

Niánlíng: 29 Diànhuà: 22166 2

Dìzhǐ: Hépíng Rd. #5

Guójí: Chinese

Zhíyè: laborer

6. Xìngmíng: Zhèng Xuéshū

Niánlíng: 21 Diànhuà: 256266

Dìzhǐ: Xuéyáng Rd. #21

Guójí: Chinese

Zhíyè: teacher

7. Xìngmíng: Zhèng Píngqiū

Niánlíng: 51 Diànhuà: 849 8888

Dìzhǐ: 8 Jīngyuán Rd.

Guójí: American (U.S.)

Zhíyè: nurse

8. Xìngmíng: Fāng Fēngmín

Niánlíng: 63 Diànhuà: 224 382

Dìzhǐ: 25 Xīnwài St.

Guójí: Japanese

Zhíyè: laborer

Unit 2h

Materials required

• Magazine cutouts/drawings of family members, pasted on 8.5" x 11" sheets of paper, with the family term written in pinyin on the reverse; enough pictures in all so that each student can have one. Make more than one example of each family member.

• Slides of members of your family. If possible, slides of members of your students' families.

• Blank 8" X 5" index cards in two colors, with an equal number of each color.

• Reprints of the masters provided.

• Unit pictures.

Introduction

• Hand out the magazine cutouts, one per student. Call out terms for family members; students holding the cards named should raise them. After a round or two, have the students exchange cards, and repeat.

• Use the instructor's set of picture cards for this lesson. Tape the picture for wo to the blackboard; then, radiating outwards from wo, introduce the other family members as you construct a family tree, taping the other pictures in place.

• Reinforce by describing relationships (Ta shi wode mama, wo shi tade nü'er; ta shi wode gege, wo shi tade meimei.)

Comprehension Drills

• Use Picture-card drills.

• Show the family slides you have available. Describe the people in the pictures; have student volunteers come to the screen and identify the people as you describe them. (Zhei shi wo baba, ta jiushi sui le. Ta pangbian de neige ren shi wo jiejie; zai ta houtou shi wo erzi.) Discuss slides of your students' families with them students ahead of time, so that you can give the introduction in class, with confirmation from the student as necessary.

• Have your students draw family trees, based on the model provided. Make a photocopy of their work, so that you have a complete set. Then have them tape their family trees to their chests. Describe elements from each student's tree ("She has two older sisters"), and have the students to who the description applies raise their hands.

• Note: Your students may have family members not listed in the vocabulary for this lesson. Examples are houfu and houmu (step-parents). Some relationships prevalent in US society are rare in Chinese, and are thus cumbersome to describe: for "my father's ex-wife," "my mother's ex-husband," or "my half-brother/half-sister" for example, no convenient equivalents exist in Chinese (<u>tongfuyimu de gege</u> for one type of half-brother is simply not convenient). If questioned, you may wish to explain this to your students. Sometimes students are reluctant to discuss their real families. If you wish, your students can each describe a fictional, idealized family.

Oral Practice

•Play "Family Feud" as follows: Fold the blank index cards in half lengthwise, one for each student in your class. Each color represents one family: the Zhang family and the Wang family. With the fold on top, write the term for one family member on the outside of each card. Include a "point-of-reference" person for each team: Zhang Xiaoying (female) for the Zhangs and Wang Xiaobo (male) for the Wangs. Remember to have only one <u>mama,</u> one <u>bàba</u> etc. per family; you can make extra brothers, sisters, aunts and uncles as necessary. Distribute one rules sheet ("Family feud") to each student, and review it with them before beginning the game.

•Have the students listen to the audiotape and complete the Dialog Practice exercise for homework. Check in class.

•Divide the class into groups of 5 to rehearse "Recognition." Have 1-2 groups perform.

•Brainstorm for variations of the sample statements and questions provided.

Controlled use
•Have your students form pairs. Distribute "A Census in China," read over the directions together, and have them complete the task assigned.

Unit 2h: Family feud

*The class divides into two teams, representing the family of **Zhāng Xiǎoyïng** (female) and the family of **Wáng Xiǎobö** (male). Team members sit side by side in one row, across from and facing the opposite team, which is also sitting in a horizontal row.*

Each student receives a "family member card." DO NOT SHOW THIS CARD TO THE OPPOSITE TEAM; place it FACING YOU on your desk.

The object of the game is for the Zhang team to guess the family identity of every member of the Wang team, and vice versa. To this end, the teams should alternate asking one question at a time of specific members of the other team. Sample questions are given below.

When a person's identity is correctly guessed, his/her card should be turned around to "reveal" it. The first team that correctly identifies all members of the opposite team first wins.

SAMPLE QUESTIONS:

Remember to use the polite form __nín__ when you address someone you think might be a generation above you—a parent, grandparent, aunt or uncle.

Nín shì nán de háishì nǔ de?	*Are you male or female?*
Nín shì lǎo rén, dà rén, háishì xiǎo háir?	*Are you an old person, an adult, or a child?*
Nǐ shì Zhāng Xiǎoyīng ma?	*Are you Zhang Xiaoying?*
Nín shì Wáng Xiǎobō de māma ma?	*Are you Wang Xiaobo's mother?*
Nǐ shì tāde gēge ma?	*Are you his brother?*

etc.

Jiā yóu!
(Go team! Rah rah.)

Unit 2h: A census in China

Imagine that you are 18 years old and living in large compound with an extended family in China. Your immediate family would occupy one wing of the compound. Imagine how many people would be in the extended family. Check off the people you select on the list provided, under "Your family." Make up ages for everyone. Note that in China you would be probably be living with your father's (rather than your mother's) relatives—China continues to be a predominantly patriarchal society. Here however we give you the option to include some maternal relations as well.

Finally, interview your partner, and take a census of his/her make-believe Chinese family.

Your family

*# of adults:*_____   *# of children:*_____

paternal grandfather _____   *age*_____   *elder brother*_____   *age*_____

*paternal grandmother*_____   *age*_____   *elder brother*_____   *age*_____

*maternal grandfather*_____   *age*_____   *elder sister*_____   *age*_____

*maternal grandmother*_____   *age*_____   *elder sister*_____   *age*_____

*paternal uncle (elder)*_____   *age*_____   *yourself*_____   *age*_____

*aunt (elder uncle's wife)*_____   *age*_____   *younger brother*_____   *age*_____

*father*_____   *age*_____   *younger brother*_____   *age*_____

*mother*_____   *age*_____   *younger sister*_____   *age*_____

*paternal uncle (younger)*_____   *age*_____   *younger sister*_____   *age*_____

*maternal aunt (mother's sister)*_____ *age*_____

Your partner's family

Duóshǎo dàrén:_____   Duóshǎo xiǎohár:_____

yéyé _____   niánlíng_____   gēge_____   niánlíng_____

nǎinai_____   niánlíng_____   gēge _____   niánlíng_____

wàigōng_____   niánlíng_____   jiějie _____   niánlíng_____

wàipó_____   niánlíng_____   jiějie_____   niánlíng_____

bófù_____   niánlíng_____   nǐ zìjǐ_____   niánlíng_____

bómǔ_____   niánlíng_____   dìdì _____   niánlíng_____

fùqīn_____   niánlíng_____   dìdì_____   niánlíng_____

mǔqīn_____   niánlíng_____   mèimèi_____   niánlíng_____

shūshu_____   niánlíng_____   mèimèi _____   niánlíng_____

āyí_____   niánlíng_____

Unit 3a

Materials required

•Class roster, one copy per student.

•One copy of the student set of picture-cards for every nine students in your class, so that each student can have one individual card at random.

•Reprints of the masters provided.

•Unit pictures.

Introduction

•Use Pantomime to introduce the vocabulary of this lesson.

Comprehension Drills

•Use Pantomime and Picture-card drills.

Oral Practice

•Distribute copies of the class roster, one per student. Cut up the copy(ies) of the student set of picture cards, and distribute one individual card at random to each student. The card that the student receives represents how that student currently "feels." Using Inner/Outer circles, have the students ASK YES/NO QUESTIONS of each other, to find out how everyone in the class is "feeling." Check everyone's "condition" on an overhead transparency when done.

•Have the students listen to the audiotape and complete the Dialog Practice exercise for homework. Check in class.

•Divide the class into groups of 3 to rehearse "Sister." Have 2-3 groups perform for the class.

•Brainstorm for variations of the sample statements and questions provided on the vocabulary sheet.

Controlled use

•Make enough copies of both handouts for "Charity," so that each student has one slip from handout one and 3-4 slips from handout two, when these are cut apart. The students are to Mingle to carry out the task on handout two. Go over the instructions with them, then distribute the slips and set the students to work. Check what each person got after everyone is done. You may wish to provide the Chinese terms for the items they received, as a preview of vocabulary from a future lesson.

Key: The Ouyang who is tired is given a chair.
The Qi who is busy is given a pen.
The Mao who is sleepy is given a pillow.
The Sun who is cold is given a sweater.
The Sun who is hot is given a fan.
The Fu who is hungry is given a bowl of noodles.
The Fu who is full is given the check for the meal.
The Wei who is thirsty is given a glass of water.
The Qi who is tired is given a bed.
The Ouyang who is busy is given a wrist-watch.
The Wei who is sleepy is given a cup of coffee.
The Zhou who is cold is given a jacket.
The Mao who is hot is given an air-conditioner.
The Ren who is hungry is given a hamburger.
The Ren who is full is given a napkin.

Unit 3a: Charity (handout #1)

Your last name is *Ōuyáng.* **You are very tired.**	Your last name is *Qí.* **You are very busy.**	Your last name is *Máo.* **You are very sleepy.**
Your last name is *Sūn.* **You are very cold.**	Your last name is *Sūn.* **You are very hot.**	Your last name is *Fù.* **You are very hungry.**
Your last name is *Fù.* **You are very full.**	Your last name is *Wèi.* **You are very thirsty.**	Your last name is *Qí.* **You are very tired.**
Your last name is *Oūyáng.* **You are very busy.**	Your last name is *Wèi.* **You are very sleepy.**	Your last name is *Zhōu.* **You are very cold.**
Your last name is *Máo.* **You are very hot.**	Your last name is *Rén.* **You are very hungry.**	Your last name is *Rén.* **You are very full.**

Unit 3a: Charity (handout #2)

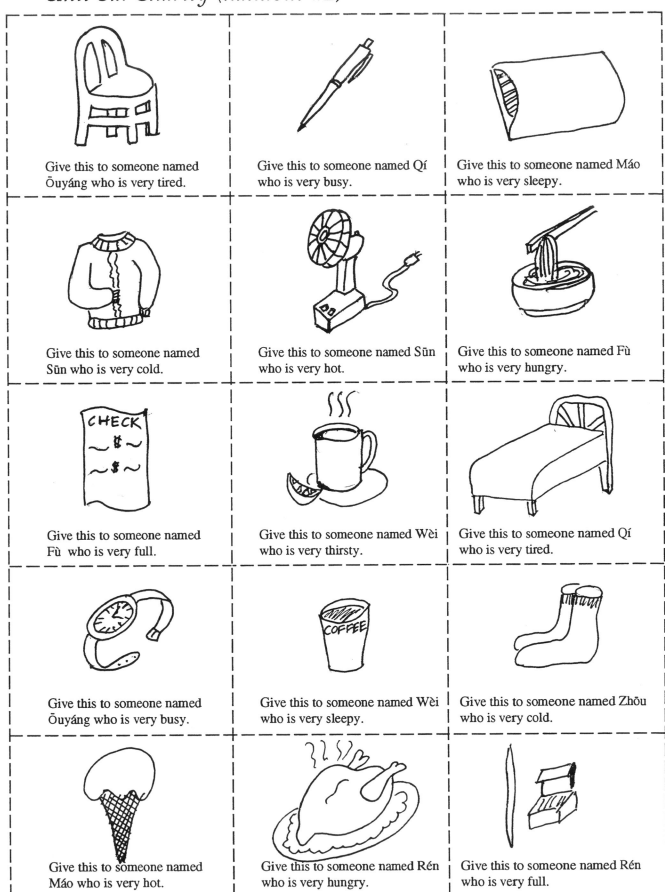

Give this to someone named Ōuyáng who is very tired.

Give this to someone named Qí who is very busy.

Give this to someone named Máo who is very sleepy.

Give this to someone named Sūn who is very cold.

Give this to someone named Sūn who is very hot.

Give this to someone named Fù who is very hungry.

Give this to someone named Fù who is very full.

Give this to someone named Wèi who is very thirsty.

Give this to someone named Qí who is very tired.

Give this to someone named Ōuyáng who is very busy.

Give this to someone named Wèi who is very sleepy.

Give this to someone named Zhōu who is very cold.

Give this to someone named Máo who is very hot.

Give this to someone named Rén who is very hungry.

Give this to someone named Rén who is very full.

Unit 3b

Materials required

•Reprints of the masters provided.

•Unit pictures.

Introduction

•Use TPR and Pantomime to introduce the actions in this lesson. Use Pantomime to introduce yao, dei, and xiang.

Comprehension Drills

•Use Pantomime and Guessing. Suggested motions for yao, dei, and xiang are folded arms or a thumping motion with a closed fist (gestures of assertion—to want to) for yao; clasped hands with interlaced fingers (a gesture of supplication—to have to) for dei; index finger to temple or hand over heart (gestures of thinking or feeling—to feel like) for xiang.

•Play Simon Says in Hungry Ghosts format with action terms. Substitute useful terms such as Qing... or Ni kuai yidiar qu... for "Simon says..."

Oral Practice

•Divide your students up into pairs or small groups of 3-4 students. One student at a time issues TPR-type commands, using his/her individual set of picture-cards as cues; the others make the appropriate motions. You may wish to set a beat (clap your hands or pound the table) for each sequence of commands-responses, beginning slowly and then moving to a quicker pace. You may wish to suggest phrases or complete sentences for the command forms, and vary them as students gain proficiency.

•Have the students listen to the audiotape and complete the Dialog Practice exercise for homework. Check in class.

•Divide the class into groups of 3 to rehearse "A Meal." Have 1-2 groups perform for the class.

•Brainstorm for variations of the sample statements and questions provided on the vocabulary sheet.

Controlled use

•Distribute one copy each of "Nosy Neighbors" to your students. Use either Mingling or Inner/outer circles to complete the task assigned. Have some of the students describe one neighbor's family as a follow-up activity.

•Have your students form pairs. Distribute one copy of "Logical Connections" to each student, and go over the instructions before setting them to work.

Unit 3b: Nosey neighbors

Pretend there are three people in your family besides you. Write who they are (eg: father, mother, sister; grandmother, uncle, aunt).

1._____ 2._____ 3._____

Pretend it is a Saturday morning at 9:00 a.m. Write what your family members are doing right now.

1._____ 2._____ 3._____

Now pretend that your classmates are your neighbors. Go to four of them, find out who the three members of their family are, and they are doing right now. Your classmates will ask the same things of you.

Neighbor 1:

Family members:

1._____ 2._____ 3._____

Activities:

1._____ 2._____ 3._____

Neighbor 2:

Family members:

1._____ 2._____ 3._____

Activities:

1._____ 2._____ 3._____

Neighbor 3:

Family members:

1._____ 2._____ 3._____

Activities:

1._____ 2._____ 3._____

Neighbor 4:

Family members:

1._____ 2._____ 3._____

Activities:

1._____ 2._____ 3._____

Unit 3b: Logical connections

What are some "causes and reactions" you've experienced? Have you ever felt like drinking some water to calm yourself down when you are frantic because you are too busy? The pictures below marked by numbers represent possible "causes," and those marked by letters represent "reactions." Write seven connections in the blanks under "Your responses" (an example is provided), and then interview your partner to find out what how he/she responded. Sequences of questions you might wish to as are <u>Nǐ xiǎng zuò shénme?</u> <u>Wèishénme?</u> and <u>Nǐ júede zěnmeyàng? Nàme nǐ xiǎng zuò shénme?</u>

Yīnwèi wǒ _____ le, suóyǐ wó xiǎng _____.

Your responses:

example: 3b

i. _____ _____
ii. _____ _____
iii. _____ _____
iv. _____ _____
v. _____ _____
vi. _____ _____
vii. _____ _____

Your partner's responses:

i. _____ _____
ii. _____ _____
iii. _____ _____
iv. _____ _____
v. _____ _____
vi. _____ _____
vii. _____ _____

Unit 4a

Materials required

• A classroom pack of **clockfaces**, one large one for the teacher and small individual ones for each of the students; either purchased from commercial suppliers of educational material, or constructed as follows.

Materials: Dinner-sized paper plate for teacher use, dessert-sized paper plates for student use; card stock; magic markers; scissors with sharp, pointed tips; round-head brass fasteners.

Procedure: Write in the numerals representing the hourly divisions on the concave side of the plates. Using the card-stock, draw and cut out short and long hands for the clockfaces. Punch holes at the base of each clockhand and at the center of each clockface with the scissors. Fasten a set of hands to each clockface with a fastener.

• Reprints of the masters provided.

Introduction

• Move the hands on the teacher's clockface into position to serve as cues to the students. Begin with yidian zhong and proceed through shi'er dian zhong, using Teacher-prompt (progressively delayed). Return to cover yidian ban, yidian yike, yidian guo wufen, etc.

Comprehension Drills

• Distribute individual clockfaces to the students. Have them manipulate them as appropriate, and proceed with Pantomime drills.

Oral Practice

• Play High/low. Use questions such as Xianzai jidian zhong? and Ni jidian zhong shuijiao? as prompts, and respond to students' guesses with zao yidiar/wan yidiar. (Zao yidiar/wan yidiar aren't actually introduced until the next lesson, but can be previewed here.)

• Have the students listen to the audiotape and complete the Dialog Practice exercise for homework. Check in class.

• Divide the class into groups of pairs to rehearse "Cramming." Have 3-4 groups perform for the class.

• Brainstorm for variations of the sample statements and questions provided on the vocabulary sheet.

Controlled use

• Distribute one copy of "Class Interview" to each student. Review the questions Ni jiao shenme mingzi? Ni jidian zhong qilai? xizao? kandianshi? shuijiao? Then have the students interview each other using the form, either by Mingling or in Inner/outer circles. They should probably interview no more than 5-10 people. To check their work, photocopy the form onto an overhead transparency, (more than one copy to accomodate a large class). Together, check each student's schedule, and write the answers on the overhead transparency.

Unit 4a: Class Interview

Interview your classmates and find out what time they do each of the activities listed below. Write their names and the times (in numerals) in the blanks provided.

Name	Get up	Take a bath	Watch TV	Go to bed
_____	_____	_____	_____	_____
_____	_____	_____	_____	_____
_____	_____	_____	_____	_____
_____	_____	_____	_____	_____
_____	_____	_____	_____	_____
_____	_____	_____	_____	_____
_____	_____	_____	_____	_____
_____	_____	_____	_____	_____
_____	_____	_____	_____	_____
_____	_____	_____	_____	_____
_____	_____	_____	_____	_____
_____	_____	_____	_____	_____
_____	_____	_____	_____	_____
_____	_____	_____	_____	_____
_____	_____	_____	_____	_____
_____	_____	_____	_____	_____
_____	_____	_____	_____	_____

Unit 4b

Materials required

• Reprints of the masters provided.

• Unit pictures.

Introduction

• Use Guessing with the picture cards.

Comprehension Drills

• China (and much of the rest of the world) uses the 24-hour clock. Drill students by writing times based on the 24-hour clock on the board (08:00; 13:24; 22:30), and having the students state the time in colloquial Chinese (zaoshang badian zhong; xiawu yidian ershi si fen; wanshang shidian ban).

Oral Practice

• Play High/low. Begin with questions such as Women shenme shihou jian? and Ni shenme shihou you kong? The answers should be times such as shangwu badian ban, xiawu wudian zhong, chi zhongfan de shihou, chi wanfan de shihou, etc. Guesses should be phrased in questions such as Shangwu xing ma? Wanshang shidian zhong xing ma? to which the teacher/student-as-teacher may respond Zao yidiar xing ma? or Wan yidiar xing ma?

• Have the students listen to the audiotape and complete the Dialog Practice exercise for homework. Check in class.

• Divide the class into pairs to rehearse "Breakfast." Have 2-3 groups perform for the class.

• Brainstorm for variations of the sample statements and questions provided on the vocabulary sheet.

Controlled use

• Have the students form pairs. One student in each pair is partner A; the other is partner B. Distribute "Making an Appointment." Brainstorm for necessary language (Ni mingtian shenme shihou you kong? Badian zhong xing ma? Liudian zhong ne?), and then have them complete the task assigned. Check to make sure each pair obtained the correct answer.

Answer: 4:00 pm to 6:00 pm

84

Unit 4b: Making an appointment (A)

Make an appointment with your partner to watch a videotape for a class project.   Find a time tomorrow (pretend it's a Saturday; follow the schedule provided below) when you both have two hours available. Suggest a time to your partner by asking, for example, "Qī diǎn zhōng xíng ma?" In response to your partner's questions, you could say either "Xíng," or "Duìbuqǐ, bùxíng. (Wǒ nèi shíhòu yǒu shì)."

6:00 *am*		**3:00** *pm*	@library ↓
7:00 *am*	Jogging ↕	**4:00** *pm*	
8:00 *am*		**5:00** *pm*	
9:00 *am*		**6:00** *pm*	movies
10:00 *am*		**7:00** *pm*	w/ C.D.
11:00 *am*		**8:00** *pm*	
12:00 *noon*		**9:00** *pm*	
1:00 *pm*		**10:00** *pm*	
2:00 *pm*	meet A.C. ↑	**11:00** *pm*	

What time tomorrow can you meet your partner?

Answer: **From** _____ *am/pm* **to** _____ *am/pm.*

Unit 4b: Making an appointment (B)

Make an appointment with your partner to watch a videotape for a class project.   Find a time tomorrow (pretend it's a Saturday; follow the schedule provided below) when you both have two hours available. Suggest a time to your partner by asking, for example, "Qī diǎn zhōng xíng ma?" In response to your partner's questions, you could say either "Xíng," or "Duìbuqǐ, bùxíng. (Wǒ nèi shíhòu yǒu shì)."

6:00 *am* ~~breakfast meeting~~	**3:00** *pm*
7:00 *am*	**4:00** *pm*
8:00 *am*	**5:00** *pm*
9:00 *am* ~~shopping w/ Dad~~	**6:00** *pm*
10:00 *am*	**7:00** *pm*
11:00 *am* ~~lunch w/ Jia ying~~	**8:00** *pm*
12:00 *noon*	**9:00** *pm* ~~overnight party @ I's house~~
1:00 *pm*	**10:00** *pm*
2:00 *pm*	**11:00** *pm*

What time tomorrow can you meet your partner?

Answer: **From** _____ *am/pm* **to** _____ *am/pm.*

Unit 4c

Materials required

•Calendar with the entire year on one page. The current year's calendar would be best, but if this is not available, then the calendar for any year would serve. The calendar should be large enough for the class to see; an alternative is to put a normal sized calendar on an overhead transparency.

•Blank 3" X 5" index cards, magic marker.

•A copy of the class roster for each student; one copy on an overhead transparency.

•Reprints of the masters provided.

Introduction

•Use Teacher prompt (progressively delayed) with the calendar as a prop.

Comprehension Drills

•Distribute seven blank 3" X 5" cards to each student. Have them write the numerals 1-6 and either tian or ri on the cards with a magic marker, to represent the days of the week. (If you wish, you can have them write tian/ri in characters; otherwise use pinyin.) Place the large calendar in clear view. Proceed with the drill by calling out dates (wuyue ershiba hao), and having the class holding up an appropriate card, depending on which day of the week the date you have given falls.

Oral Practice

•Hand out a copy of the class roster to each student. Have them find out the birthdays of their classmates, including year-month-day, either by Mingling or Inner-outer circles. After everyone is done, check the birthdays on an overhead transparency.

•Have the students Line-up by order of their birthday.

•Have the students listen to the audiotape and complete the Dialog Practice exercise for homework. Check in class.

•Divide the class into groups of 5 to rehearse "The Zodiac." Have 1-2 groups perform for the class.

•Brainstorm for variations of the sample statements and questions provided on the vocabulary sheet.

Controlled use

•Divide the students into pairs, and have them do the pair work exercise entitled "Long-range plans," using copies of the masters provided. Check to make sure each pair obtains the correct answer.

Answer: February 25, 2055

Unit 4c: Long-range plans (A)

Following are make-believe calendars for three years. Pretend that you and your partner are both extremely busy people. The dates circled are days when you are not working. Make an appointment with your partner to spend a day together, sometime in those three years. Remember, however, that you play golf every Wednesday and Friday.

2054

	M T W Th F Sa Su M T W Th F Sa Su M T W Th F Sa Su M T W
January	1 2 3 4 (5 6 7 8 9) 10 11 12 13 14 15 16 17 18 19 20 21 22 23 24 25 26 27 (28 29 30) 31
February	1 2 3 4 5 6 7 8 9 10 11 12 13 14 15 16 17 18 19 20 21 22 23 24 25 26 27 28
March	1 2 3 4 5 6 7 8 9 10 11 12 13 14 15 16 17 18 19 20 21 (22 23) 24 25 26 27 28 29 30 31
April	1 2 3 4 5 6 7 8 9 10 11 12 13 (14) 15 16 17 18 19 20 21 22 23 24 25 26 27 28 29 30
May	1 2 3 4 5 6 7 8 9 10 11 12 13 14 15 16 17 18 19 20 21 22 23 24 25 (26 27 28 29 30) 31
June	1 2 3 4 5 6 7 8 9 10 11 (12 13 14 15 16) 17 18 19 20 21 22 23 24 25 26 27 28 29 30
July	1 2 (3 4 5 6) 7 8 9 10 11 12 13 14 15 16 17 18 19 20 21 22 23 24 25 26 27 28 29 30 31
August	1 2 3 4 5 6 7 8 9 10 11 12 13 (14 15) 16 17 18 19 20 21 22 23 24 25 26 27 28 29 30 31
September	1 2 3 4 5 6 7 8 9 10 11 12 13 14 15 16 17 18 19 20 21 22 23 (24 25 26 27 28 29) 30
October	1 2 3 4 5 6 7 8 9 10 11 12 13 14 15 16 17 (18 19) 20 21 22 23 24 25 26 27 28 29 30 31
November	1 2 3 4 5 (6 7 8 9) 10 11 12 13 14 15 16 17 18 19 20 21 22 23 24 25 26 27 28 29 30
December	1 2 3 4 5 6 7 8 9 10 11 12 13 14 15 16 17 18 19 20 21 22 23 24 25 (26 27 28 29) 30 31

2055

	M T W Th F Sa Su M T W Th F Sa Su M T W Th F Sa Su M T W
January	(1 2 3 4 5) 6 7 8 9 10 11 12 (13) 14 15 16 17 18 19 20 21 22 23 24 25 26 27 28 29 30 31
February	1 2 3 4 5 6 7 8 9 10 11 12 13 14 15 16 17 18 19 20 21 22 23 24 (25 26 27 28)
March	1 2 3 4 5 6 7 8 9 10 11 12 13 14 15 16 17 18 (19 20 21) 22 23 24 25 26 27 28 29 30 31
April	1 2 3 4 5 6 7 8 9 10 11 12 13 14 15 16 17 18 19 20 21 22 23 24 (25 26) 27 28 29 30
May	1 2 3 4 5 6 7 8 9 10 11 (12 13 14 15 16) 17 18 19 20 21 22 23 24 25 26 27 (28 29) 30 31
June	1 2 3 4 5 6 7 8 9 10 11 12 13 14 15 16 17 18 19 20 21 (22) 23 24 25 26 27 28 29 30
July	1 2 3 4 5 6 7 8 9 10 11 12 13 14 15 16 17 18 19 20 21 22 23 24 25 26 27 28 (29 30) 31
August	1 2 3 4 5 6 7 8 9 10 11 12 13 14 15 16 17 18 19 20 (21 22) 23 24 25 26 27 28 29 30 31
September	1 2 3 4 5 (6 7 8 9 10 11) 12 13 14 15 16 17 18 19 20 21 22 23 24 25 26 27 28 29 30
October	1 2 3 4 5 6 7 8 9 10 11 12 13 14 15 16 17 18 19 20 21 (22 23 24) 25 26 27 28 29 30 31
November	1 2 3 4 5 6 7 8 9 10 11 12 13 14 15 16 17 18 19 20 21 22 23 24 25 (26) 27 28 29 30
December	1 2 3 4 5 6 7 8 9 10 11 12 13 14 (15 16) 17 18 19 20 21 22 23 24 25 26 27 28 29 30 31

2056

	M T W Th F Sa Su M T W Th F Sa Su M T W Th F Sa Su M T W
January	(1 2 3 4 5) 6 7 8 9 10 11 12 13 14 15 16 17 18 19 20 21 22 23 24 25 (26 27 28 29 30) 31
February	1 2 3 4 5 6 7 8 9 10 11 12 13 14 15 16 17 (18 19 20) 21 22 23 24 25 26 27 28
March	1 2 3 4 5 6 7 8 9 10 11 12 13 14 15 16 17 18 19 20 21 22 23 24 25 26 27 28 29 30 31
April	1 2 3 4 5 6 7 8 9 10 11 (12 13 14 15 16) 17 18 19 20 21 22 23 24 25 26 27 28 29 30
May	1 2 3 4 5 6 7 8 9 10 11 12 13 14 15 16 17 18 19 20 (21 22) 23 24 25 26 27 28 29 30 31
June	1 2 3 4 5 6 7 8 9 10 11 12 13 14 15 16 17 18 19 20 21 22 23 24 25 (26 27 28 29 30)
July	(1 2 3 4) 5 6 7 8 9 10 11 12 13 14 15 16 17 18 19 20 21 22 23 24 25 26 27 28 29 30 31
August	1 2 3 4 5 6 7 8 9 10 11 12 13 14 15 16 17 18 19 20 21 22 23 24 25 26 27 28 29 30 31
September	1 2 3 4 5 6 7 8 9 (10 11 12) 13 14 15 16 17 18 19 20 21 22 23 24 25 26 27 28 29 30
October	1 2 3 4 5 6 7 8 9 10 11 12 13 14 15 16 17 18 19 20 21 22 23 24 25 26 27 28 29 30 31
November	1 2 3 4 5 6 7 8 9 10 11 12 13 14 15 16 17 18 (19 20 21) 22 23 24 25 26 27 (28 29 30)
December	1 2 3 4 5 6 7 8 9 10 11 (12 13 14 15 16) 17 18 19 20 21 22 23 24 25 26 27 28 29 30 31

ANSWER:_____

(write date)

Unit 4c: Long-range plans (B)

Following are make-believe calendars for three years. Pretend that you and your partner are both extremely busy people. The dates circled are days when you are not working. Make an appointment with your partner to spend a day together, sometime in those three years. Remember, however, that you visit your uncle every Tuesday.

2054

	M T W Th F Sa Su M T W Th F Sa Su M T W Th F Sa Su M T W Th F Sa Su M T W
January	(1 2) 3 4 5 6 7 8 9 10 11 12 13 14 15 (16 17 18 19) 20 21 22 23 24 25 26 27 28 29 30 31
February	1 2 3 4 5 6 (7 8 9 10 11 12) 13 14 15 16 17 18 19 20 21 22 23 24 25 26 27 28
March	1 2 3 4 5 6 7 8 9 10 11 12 13 14 (15 16 17) 18 19 20 21 22 23 24 25 26 27 28 29 30 31
April	1 2 3 4 5 6 7 8 9 10 11 12 13 14 15 16 17 18 19 20 21 22 23 24 25 26 27 28 29 30
May	1 2 3 4 5 (6 7 8 9 10 11) 12 13 14 15 16 17 18 19 20 21 22 23 24 25 26 27 28 29 30 31
June	1 2 3 4 5 6 7 8 9 10 11 12 13 14 15 16 17 18 19 20 21 22 23 24 25 26 27 28 29 30
July	(1 2 3) 4 5 6 7 8 9 10 11 12 13 14 15 16 17 18 19 20 21 22 23 24 25 26 27 28 29 30 31
August	1 2 3 4 5 6 7 8 9 10 11 12 13 14 15 16 17 18 19 20 (21 22 23 24) 25 26 27 28 29 30 31
September	1 2 3 4 5 6 7 (8) 9 10 11 12 13 14 15 16 17 18 19 20 21 22 23 24 25 26 27 28 29 30
October	1 2 3 4 5 6 7 8 9 (10 11 12 13) 14 15 16 17 18 19 20 21 22 23 24 25 26 27 28 29 30 31
November	1 2 3 4 5 6 7 8 9 10 11 12 13 14 15 (16 17 18) 19 20 21 22 23 24 25 26 27 28 29 30
December	1 2 3 4 5 6 7 8 9 10 11 12 13 14 15 16 17 18 19 20 21 22 (23 24 25) 26 27 28 29 30 31

2055

	M T W Th F Sa Su M T W Th F Sa Su M T W Th F Sa Su M T W Th F Sa Su M T W
January	1 2 3 4 (5 6 7) 8 9 10 11 12 13 14 15 16 17 18 19 20 21 22 23 24 25 26 27 28 29 30 31
February	1 2 3 4 5 6 7 8 9 10 11 12 13 14 15 16 17 18 19 20 21 22 (23 24 25) 26 27 28
March	1 2 3 4 5 6 (7 8 9 10 11 12 13) 14 15 16 17 18 19 20 21 22 23 24 25 26 27 28 29 30 31
April	(1 2 3 4 5) 6 7 8 9 10 11 12 13 14 15 16 17 18 19 20 21 22 23 24 25 26 27 28 29 30
May	1 2 3 4 5 6 7 8 9 10 11 12 13 14 15 16 17 18 19 20 (21 22 23) 24 25 26 27 28 29 30 31
June	1 2 3 4 5 6 7 (8 9 10 11) 12 13 14 15 16 17 18 19 20 21 22 23 24 25 26 27 28 29 30
July	1 2 3 4 5 6 7 8 9 10 11 12 13 (14 15 16) 17 18 19 20 21 22 23 24 25 26 27 28 29 30 31
August	1 2 3 (4 5 6 7 8 9) 10 11 12 13 14 15 16 17 18 19 20 21 22 23 24 25 26 27 28 29 30 31
September	1 2 3 4 5 6 7 8 9 (10) 11 12 13 14 15 16 17 18 19 20 21 22 23 24 25 26 27 28 29 30
October	1 2 3 4 5 6 7 8 9 10 11 12 13 14 15 16 17 18 19 20 21 22 23 (24 25 26 27 28 29 30) 31
November	1 2 3 4 5 6 (7) 8 9 10 11 12 13 14 15 16 17 18 19 20 21 22 23 24 25 26 27 28 29 30
December	1 2 3 4 5 6 7 8 9 10 11 12 13 14 15 (16 17) 18 19 20 21 22 23 24 (25 26) 27 28 29 30 31

2056

	M T W Th F Sa Su M T W Th F Sa Su M T W Th F Sa Su M T W Th F Sa Su M T W
January	1 2 3 4 5 6 7 8 9 10 11 12 13 14 (15 16) 17 18 19 20 21 22 23 24 25 26 27 28 29 (30 31)
February	1 2 3 (4 5 6) 7 8 9 10 11 12 13 14 15 16 17 18 19 20 21 22 23 24 25 26 27 28
March	1 2 3 4 5 6 7 8 9 10 11 12 13 14 15 16 17 18 19 20 21 22 23 24 25 26 27 28 29 30 31
April	1 2 3 4 (5) 6 7 8 9 10 11 12 13 14 15 16 17 18 19 20 21 22 23 24 25 26 27 28 29 30
May	1 2 3 4 5 6 7 8 9 10 11 12 13 14 15 16 17 18 19 20 21 22 (23) 24 25 26 27 28 29 30 31
June	1 2 3 4 5 6 7 8 9 10 11 12 13 14 15 16 17 18 19 20 21 22 (23 24) 25 26 27 28 29 30
July	1 2 3 4 5 6 7 8 9 (10 11 12) 13 14 15 16 17 18 19 20 21 22 23 24 25 26 27 28 29 30 31
August	1 2 3 4 5 6 7 8 9 10 11 12 13 14 15 16 17 18 19 20 21 (22) 23 24 25 26 27 28 29 30 31
September	1 2 3 4 5 (6 7 8 9 10) 11 12 13 14 15 16 17 18 19 20 21 22 23 24 25 26 27 28 29 30
October	1 2 3 4 5 6 7 8 9 10 11 12 13 14 15 16 17 (18 19) 20 21 22 23 24 25 26 27 28 29 30 31
November	1 2 3 4 5 6 (7 8) 9 10 11 12 13 14 15 16 17 18 19 20 21 22 23 24 25 26 27 28 29 30
December	1 2 3 4 5 6 7 8 9 10 11 12 13 14 15 (16 17 18 19 20) 21 22 23 24 25 26 27 28 29 30 31

ANSWER:_____

(write date)

Unit 4d

Materials required

•Blank 3" X 5" index cards, 7 for each student; "magic" marking pens.

•Current month's calendar (may be on an overhead transparency)

•Reprints of the masters provided.

Introduction

•*Introducing "day before yesterday," "yesterday," "today," "tomorrow," "day after tomorrow":*
Write today's date on the blackboard (or point to it on the calendar), and say Jintian shi
(..nian...yue...hao/ri). Repeat, while urging the students to guess the meaning of what you
have said. Repeat the process for qiantian (point to or write the date of two days ago),
zuotian (point to or write yesterday's date), mingtian (point to or write tomorrow's date), and
houtian (point to or write day after tomorrow's date).

•*Introducing "in the past" and "in the future":* Reinforce xianzai by having the students
respond to Xianzai jidian zhong? Then indicate today's date and say Jintian shi xianzai.
Indicate all dates before today and say Zhe shi yiqian. Indicate all dates after today and say
Zhe shi yihou. (Repeat each of the statements until all students indicate that they understand
what you mean.)

•*Introducing "two days ago," "a week ago," two days from now," "one week from now," "last week,"
"this week," and "next week."* Use the calendar. Point to (or draw a line around) the day or
week in question and say liang tian yiqian, or Zhe shi liang tian yiqian; shangge xingqi or
Zhe shi shangge xingqi; etc.

Comprehension Drills

•Distribute seven blank 3" X 5" cards to each student. Have them write the numerals 1-6 and
either tian or ri on the cards with a magic marker, to represent the days of the week. (If you
wish, you can have them write tian/ri in characters; otherwise use pinyin.) [These cards were
used in Unit 4c as well; you may wish to re-use them.] Proceed with the drill by dalling out
specific days (jintian, mingtian, liangtian yihou), and having the class identify them by
holding up appropriate cards.

Oral Practice

•Make one copy of "Have you seen *Gone with the Wind?*" Cut apart the slips provided,
distribute one each at random to the students, and play Lineup. They are to ask their classmates the question Ni kan guo *Gone with the Wind* ma? (substitute the name of a current box-
office hit, if you wish). The time expression on the slip each student is holding represents the

time when s/he saw or will see the movie. If the expression on the slip indicates the past, the student being interviewed should respond Kan guo le, whereupon the interviewer should follow up with Shenme shihou kan de? and the response should be the time expression on the interviewee's cue slip. If the expression indicates the future, the response should be Haimei kan, to be followed by the question Shenme shihou yao kan? etc. The goal of the activity is to have the students find out when everyone in the class "saw" or "will see" *Gone with the Wind*, and line themselves up accordingly, from the earliest to the latest.

• Have the students listen to the audiotape and complete the Dialog Practice exercise for homework. Check in class.

• Divide the class into groups of 5 to rehearse "An Appointment." Have 1 group perform.

• Brainstorm for variations of the sample statements and questions provided.

Controlled use

• Have the students form pairs. One in each is partner A, the other is partner B. Distribute the worksheets for "Catching an error," and read them the directions. Brainstorm for what they would have to say to complete the task. (Q: Ni jintian kanle shei? Zuotian you ren laile ma? Qiantian ne? Mingtian ne? A: Wo zuotian kanle X xiansheng. Qiantian meiyou ren lai, wutian yiqian Y xiaojie lai le.), then let them begin. Check to make sure each pair obtains the correct answer.

Correct Answer: Zhao and Liu were incorrectly scheduled.

Unit 4d: Have you seen _Gone with the Wind?_

sāntiān yǐqián	wǔtiān yǐhòu	yíge xīngqī yǐqián
liǎngge xīngqī yǐqián	qiántiān	sānge xīngqī yǐqián
liǎngtiān yǐqián	shàngge xīngqī	jīntiān
zuótiān	sìtiān yǐqián	liǎngtiān yǐhòu
sìtiān yǐqián	sāntiān yǐhòu	xiàge xīngqī
sìge xīngqī yǐhòu	míngtiān	liǎngge xīngqī yǐhòu
sìtiān yǐhòu	sānge xīngqī yǐhòu	hòutiān

Unit 4d: Catching an error (A)

You and your partner are lab technicians working in two different hospitals in a Chinese community. The following is your schedule of appointments for three weeks: each cell in the three columns below represent one day. **The day marked with an asterisk is today.** *Each name represents a person who has made an appointment with you to have a blood sample taken. These same people have made appointments with your partner as well, to have a second sample taken. The two samples from each person must be taken on different days. As you see from the calendar below, you have already taken several samples. At the end of the day today, however, the scheduling clerk comes rushing to you in a panic: he has erroneously scheduled a number of people to have their samples drawn on the same day. Pretend you are now on the telephone to your partner. Discuss your schedules, and discover which patients had or are scheduled to have their blood taken by the two of you on the same day.*

Week one	Week two	Week three
Chen		*Li*
	Wang	Bai
Zhao	*WU	
Yang		
	Pang	Liu
		Zhang

Names of patients erroneously scheduled: _____

Unit 4d: Catching an error (B)

You and your partner are lab technicians working in two different hospitals in a Chinese community. The following is your schedule of appointments for three weeks: each cell in the three columns below represent one day. **The day marked with an asterisk is today.** *Each name represents a person who has made an appointment with you to have a blood sample taken. These same people have made appointments with your partner as well, to have a second sample taken. The two samples from each person must be taken on different days. As you see from the calendar below, you have already taken several samples. At the end of the day today, however, the scheduling clerk comes rushing to you in a panic: he has erroneously scheduled a number of people to have their samples drawn on the same day. Pretend you are now on the telephone to your partner. Discuss your schedules, and discover which patients had or are scheduled to have their blood taken by the two of you on the same day.*

Week one	Week two	Week three
Li		*Chen*
Bai	Wu	
Zhao	*WANG	
		Yang
Pang		Liu
	Zhang	

Names of patients erroneously scheduled: _____

Unit 4e

Materials required

•Blank 3" X 5" index cards in two to four colors, approximately 25 of each color, depending on the size of your class. (Provide one set of 25 cards for each multiple of 5 students in your class. For fifteen or sixteen students, for example, provide 75 cards in three colors—3 sets of 25, each set of a different color.) Magic markers.
•Current year's calendar, preferably on one sheet of paper. (May be on an overhead transparency.)
•Reprints of the masters provided.
•Unit pictures.

Introduction

•*Introducing "two months ago, last month....:"*

Use the calendar. Point to (or draw a line around) the current month, and say <u>zheige yue</u>. Proceed with each of the other months, and repeat, using Teacher prompt (progressively delayed).

•*Introducing the years:*

Write the current year (say, 1992) on an index card. On six additional index cards, write three years into the future and three years into the past (say, 1993, 1994, and 1995, and 1989, 1990, and 1991). Hold up the card for the current year and say <u>jinnian</u>. Proceed with each of the other years (<u>mingnian</u>, <u>liangnian yihou</u>, etc.). Repeat, using Teacher prompt (progressively delayed).

•*Introducing the seasons:*

Use either Pantomime, or the picture cards provided.

Comprehension Drills

•Divide your class into groups of approximately five. Distribute one set of cards to each group; make sure that the groups have cards of different colors. (Thus, the class may be divided into the blue group, the white group, the yellow group, etc., depending on the color of the cards they have.) Distribute magic markers. Have someone in each group write first the numbers 1-12 and then the years you are drilling (say 1987-1993) on individual index cards. Also have someone in each group either write the Chinese characters <u>chun, xia, qiu, dong</u> on index cards, or cut out and paste down the picture cards for each of the seasons. Proceed with the Card toss game.

Oral Practice

•Make one copy of "Have you read *War and Peace?*"   Cut apart the slips provided, distribute one each at random to the students, and play Lineup. They are to ask their classmates the question <u>Ni kan guo *War and Peace* ma?</u> (substitute the name of a relevant book, or of the Chinese classic novel *The Dream of the Red Chamber* (<u>Honglou Meng</u>), if you wish). The time expression on the slip each student is holding represents the time when s/he read or will read the book. If the expression on the slip indicates the past, the student being interviewed should respond <u>Kan guo le</u>, whereupon the interviewer should follow up with <u>Shenme shihou kan de?</u> and the response should be the time expression on the interviewee's cue slip. If the expression indicates the future, the response should be <u>Haimei kan</u>, to be followed by the question <u>Shenme shihou yao kan?</u> etc. The goal of the activity is to have the students find out when everyone in the class "read" or "will read" *War and Peace*, and line themselves up accordingly, from the earliest to the latest.

•Have the students listen to the audiotape and complete the Dialog Practice exercise for homework. Check in class.

•Divide the class into groups of 5 to rehearse "At Wu's House." Have 1-2 groups perform for the class.

•Brainstorm for variations of the sample statements and questions provided on the vocabulary sheet.

Controlled use

•Distribute one copy of "The new car" to each student. Brainstorm for necessary language (Ni shi neinian maide che? Shi chuntian maide ma? Shi neige yue maide?), and then have them complete the task assigned. Use either Mingling or Inner/outer circles. After everyone is done, compile a complete roster of everyone's dates of purchase on a overhead transparency.

Unit 4e: Have you read War and Peace ?

jīntiān	míngtiān	hòutiān
qiántiān	zuótiān	sāntiān yǐqián
sāntiān yǐhòu	sìtiān yǐqián	sìtiān yǐhòu
shàngge xīngqī	xiàge xīngqī	liǎngge xīngqī yǐqián
liǎngge xīngqī yǐhòu	shàngge yuè	xiàge yuè
sānge yuè yǐqián	sānge yuè yǐhòu	wǔge yuè yǐqián
sìge yuè yǐqián	sìge yuè yǐhòu	liùge yuè yǐqián
liùge yuè yǐhòu	míngnián	qùnián
liǎngnián yǐqián	liǎngnián yǐhòu	sānnián yǐhòu
sānnián yǐqián	wǔnián yǐqián	sìnián yǐhòu

Unit 4e: The new car

Step 1: *Pretend that you recently bought (or plan to soon buy) a new car. Make up a date of purchase by circling the year, the season, and the month in the choices listed below.*

3 yrs ago / 2 yrs ago / last year / this year / next year / 2 yrs from now / 3 yrs from now

Spring Summer Fall Winter

January February March April May June July August September October November December

Step 2: *Interview your classmates and find out when they purchased their cars.*

Name	Year	Season	Month
_____	_____	_____	_____
_____	_____	_____	_____
_____	_____	_____	_____
_____	_____	_____	_____
_____	_____	_____	_____
_____	_____	_____	_____
_____	_____	_____	_____
_____	_____	_____	_____
_____	_____	_____	_____
_____	_____	_____	_____
_____	_____	_____	_____
_____	_____	_____	_____

Unit 5a

Materials required

• One or more sets of US play currency (available from educational materials stores).

• Real Chinese currency, if available.

• A serving tray.

• One pack of playing cards per eight students in your class, separated into suites. Discard Queens, Kings, and Jokers.

• Reprints of the masters provided.

Introduction

• Distribute play money in each of the denominations to your students. Using Guessing, introduce terms for monetary units.

Comprehension Drills

• Place your sets of play money on a tray. Go around the room, offer the tray to each student, and specify that they take a certain amount of money. (Qing na wukuai qian. Qing na qikuai wumao qian. Qing na jiumao jiufen qian. etc.) If your class is small enough, you may wish to go around more than once.

• Collect the money back from the students by the same process. Tell the students they should try to "spend" all the money they are holding as soon as possible. Call out a random amount, and collect it from the first student who holds up the correct currency. Continue until all money has been collected. Applaud each time a student has given up all their cash.

• Alternatively, distribute a set amount of money to each student. Call out random amounts and have them display the correct currency in response.

• Distribute one authentic Chinese coin or bill to each student; call out a denomination, and have the student holding it raise it up. After a round or two, have the students exchange the money with someone else, and repeat the drill.

Oral Practice

• Form the students into pairs, distribute one suite of playing cards (Ace to 10) per pair. Have them practice stating amounts using the Card drill.

• Distribute one blank index card to each student. Have them write any amount up to $50.00 on their index card; the card will represent something they are offering for sale at the amount they have written down. Distribute a copy of the class roster to each student. Using Mingling or Inner/outer circles, have the students find out from everyone one in the class the price of the "items" (Q: "Zheige duoshao qian?" A: "Qikuai jiumao jiu.")

• Have the students listen to the audiotape and complete the Dialog Practice exercise for homework. Check in class.

• Break the class into pairs to rehearse "Comparisons." Have 1-2 groups perform.

• Brainstorm for variations of the sample statements and questions provided.

Controlled use

•Divide your class into two groups, the "buyers" and the "sellers." It doesn't matter if the groups are slightly uneven. Give $10 (a five and five singles) to each of the buyers, and $5 (three singles and $2 in change) to each of the sellers, so that they can make change.

Cut apart "Shopping for numbers" on the dotted line, and distribute a copy of the top (seller's) portion to each seller, and a copy of the bottom (buyer's) portion to each buyer. Make sure everyone understand the directions. Seat the sellers (preferably in a circle of chairs), and allow the buyers to move freely among them. Encourage the buyers to try more than one seller to get what they want.

After a set period of time (approximately 15 minutes), call the activity off and check to see 1) which seller has made the most money; 2) which buyers have gotten a complete set of the numbers 1-4; and 3) which buyers have spent the least money. Congratulate students as appropriate.

Unit 5a: Shopping for numbers (Seller)

Pretend you sell the numbers 1-4. (Personalize your goods for sale by signing your name on the lines below. Then [carefully!] tear them apart.) Your customers each have $10 to spend, and they want to buy the numbers 1-4. Make as much money as you can by selling what you have. Decide the price of each of your numbers, and then try to keep the price high as you haggle with the buyer. Don't set your price so high that you lose your sale, though!

You start off with $5 in bills and change. Write the total amount you have at the end of the activity here:

_____

- -

The number "1," manufactured by
_____ Price: _____

- -

The number "2," manufactured by
_____ Price: _____

- -

The number "3," manufactured by
_____ Price: _____

- -

The number "4," manufactured by
_____ Price: _____

■ ■

Unit 5a: Shopping for numbers (Buyer)

You need to buy one complete set of the numbers 1-4. You do not want any duplicate numbers. You have $10 to spend. Go to any of the sellers available, and try to spend as little as possible to buy what you must. Haggle with the sellers; of course, they intend to make as much as they can from you.

Write here how much money you have left after you have made your purchases.

Unit 5b

Materials required

•One set of shapes, constructed as follows.

Materials: Several sheets of contruction or artist's colored paper in red, blue, and white; scissors; access to lamination.

Procedure: 1) Cut out one large red circle (say 5" in diameter), one medium red circle (say 3" in diameter), and one small red circle (say 1" in diameter). 2) Repeat Step1 using the colors blue and white. 3) Repeat Steps 1 and 2 for squares, rectangles, and triangles. You will end up with a set of 36 shapes. Laminate them for protection.

•Set of play money.

•Reprints of the masters provided.

Introduction

Use Guessing and the instructor sets of the shapes to introduce the vocabulary in this lesson.

Comprehension Drills

•Use Picture-card drills, substituting the shapes for pictures.

•Brainstorm for variations of the sample statements and questions provided on the vocabulary sheet.

Oral Practice

•Have each student take out a book or notebook, and open it to any page. Walk around the class and slip one shape card at random into each book, so that the student but not his/her classmates see the card. Using Inner/outer circles, have the students interview each other to determine which card each is holding. The students may not see each other's cards, and may not make any notes. They may interview any student more than once.

When they are done, have them take seats, preferably in a circle or a U-shape. Ask individuals to fetch certain shapes to you ("Qing ba xiao hong yuanquan gei wo"). The student called upon must go to a classmate and request "Qing ba xiao hong yuanquan gei wo." The better his/her memory, the fewer classmates he/she will have to approach. Continue for approximately 10 minutes, or until all shapes have been collected.

•Have the students listen to the audiotape and complete the Dialog Practice exercise for homework. Check in class.

•Break the class into groups of 4 to rehearse "A New Baby." Have 1-2 groups perform for the class.

•Brainstorm for variations of the sample statements and questions provided.

Controlled use

•Divide your class into two groups, the "buyers" and the "sellers." It doesn't matter if the groups are slightly uneven. Give $10 (a five and five singles) to each of the buyers, and $5 (three singles and $2 in change) to each of the sellers, so that they can make change.

Distribute your laminated shapes as evenly as you can among your sellers.

Make copies of "Shopping for shapes (Buyer)" and "Shopping for shapes (Seller)" and cut them apart. (Each page has six slips on it, so you probably won't need to make more than 3-4 copies of the page.) Distribute one "buyer's" slip to each "buyer" and one "seller's" slip to each "seller." Make sure everyone understand the directions. Seat the sellers (preferably in a circle of chairs), and allow the buyers to move freely among them. Encourage the buyers to try more than one seller to get what they want.

After a set period of time (approximately 15 minutes), call the activity off and check to see 1) which seller has made the most money; 2) which buyers have gotten a complete set of shapes as specified; and 3) which buyers have spent the least money. Congratulate students as appropriate.

104

Unit 5b: Shopping for shapes (Seller)

You have a number of shapes to sell. The buyers will have $10 each to spend on four items. Decide how much you want to get for each of your shapes, then try to keep your prices high as you haggle with the buyers. However, if your prices are too high, you won't be able to keep buyers, so be careful.

Unit 5b: Shopping for shapes (Seller)

You have a number of shapes to sell. The buyers will have $10 each to spend on four items. Decide how much you want to get for each of your shapes, then try to keep your prices high as you haggle with the buyers. However, if your prices are too high, you won't be able to keep buyers, so be careful.

Unit 5b: Shopping for shapes (Seller)

You have a number of shapes to sell. The buyers will have $10 each to spend on four items. Decide how much you want to get for each of your shapes, then try to keep your prices high as you haggle with the buyers. However, if your prices are too high, you won't be able to keep buyers, so be careful.

Unit 5b: Shopping for shapes (Seller)

You have a number of shapes to sell. The buyers will have $10 each to spend on four items. Decide how much you want to get for each of your shapes, then try to keep your prices high as you haggle with the buyers. However, if your prices are too high, you won't be able to keep buyers, so be careful.

Unit 5b: Shopping for shapes (Seller)

You have a number of shapes to sell. The buyers will have $10 each to spend on four items. Decide how much you want to get for each of your shapes, then try to keep your prices high as you haggle with the buyers. However, if your prices are too high, you won't be able to keep buyers, so be careful.

Unit 5b: Shopping for shapes (Seller)

You have a number of shapes to sell. The buyers will have $10 each to spend on four items. Decide how much you want to get for each of your shapes, then try to keep your prices high as you haggle with the buyers. However, if your prices are too high, you won't be able to keep buyers, so be careful.

Unit 5b: Shopping for shapes (Buyer)

You need to buy four items: one circle, one triangle, one square, and one rectangle. Together they must include at least one each of the three sizes and at least one each of the three colors, in any combination that you like. In other words, buy at least one large shape, one medium shape, and one small shape; and at least one red shape, one blue shape, and one white shape.

You have $10. Try to spend as little as possible, and still get what you need. You are welcome to try more than one seller to get an appropriate combination of shapes at a suitable price.

Unit 5b: Shopping for shapes (Buyer)

You need to buy four items: one circle, one triangle, one square, and one rectangle. Together they must include at least one each of the three sizes and at least one each of the three colors, in any combination that you like. In other words, buy at least one large shape, one medium shape, and one small shape; and at least one red shape, one blue shape, and one white shape.

You have $10. Try to spend as little as possible, and still get what you need. You are welcome to try more than one seller to get an appropriate combination of shapes at a suitable price.

Unit 5b: Shopping for shapes (Buyer)

You need to buy four items: one circle, one triangle, one square, and one rectangle. Together they must include at least one each of the three sizes and at least one each of the three colors, in any combination that you like. In other words, buy at least one large shape, one medium shape, and one small shape; and at least one red shape, one blue shape, and one white shape.

You have $10. Try to spend as little as possible, and still get what you need. You are welcome to try more than one seller to get an appropriate combination of shapes at a suitable price.

Unit 5b: Shopping for shapes (Buyer)

You need to buy four items: one circle, one triangle, one square, and one rectangle. Together they must include at least one each of the three sizes and at least one each of the three colors, in any combination that you like. In other words, buy at least one large shape, one medium shape, and one small shape; and at least one red shape, one blue shape, and one white shape.

You have $10. Try to spend as little as possible, and still get what you need. You are welcome to try more than one seller to get an appropriate combination of shapes at a suitable price.

Unit 5b: Shopping for shapes (Buyer)

You need to buy four items: one circle, one triangle, one square, and one rectangle. Together they must include at least one each of the three sizes and at least one each of the three colors, in any combination that you like. In other words, buy at least one large shape, one medium shape, and one small shape; and at least one red shape, one blue shape, and one white shape.

You have $10. Try to spend as little as possible, and still get what you need. You are welcome to try more than one seller to get an appropriate combination of shapes at a suitable price.

Unit 5b: Shopping for shapes (Buyer)

You need to buy four items: one circle, one triangle, one square, and one rectangle. Together they must include at least one each of the three sizes and at least one each of the three colors, in any combination that you like. In other words, buy at least one large shape, one medium shape, and one small shape; and at least one red shape, one blue shape, and one white shape.

You have $10. Try to spend as little as possible, and still get what you need. You are welcome to try more than one seller to get an appropriate combination of shapes at a suitable price.

Unit 5c

Materials required
• Reprints of the masters provided.

• Unit pictures.

Introduction
• Use Guessing with the unit pictures.

Comprehension Drills
• Use Picture-card drills.

Oral Practice
• Have the students form pairs. Distribute a set of "What do you have?" (A and B forms) to each pair, and have them complete the task assigned.

• Have the students listen to the audiotape and complete the Dialog Practice exercise for homework. Check in class.

• Break the class into groups of 5 to rehearse "A Gift for the Baby." Have 2-3 groups perform for the class.

• Brainstorm for variations of the sample statements and questions provided on the vocabulary sheet.

Controlled use
• Divide the students into groups of three or four. Distribute forms A-D of "Rummage Sale," one set to each group, and have them complete the task assigned. When all groups are done, check together for the lowest available price of all items.

Unit 5c: What do you have? (A)

The following are items you have in your possession. Compare your store with your partner's WITHOUT LOOKING AT HIS/HER PICTURE. Find out how many of each item your partner has, and record the number in the spaces provided.

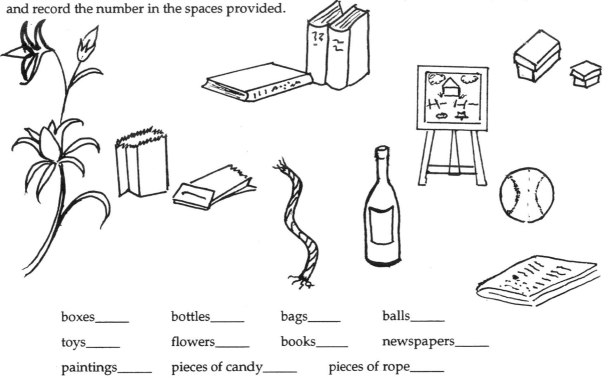

boxes_____   bottles_____   bags_____   balls_____

toys_____   flowers_____   books_____   newspapers_____

paintings_____   pieces of candy_____   pieces of rope_____

- -

Unit 5c: What do you have? (B)

The following are items you have in your possession. Compare your store with your partner's WITHOUT LOOKING AT HIS/HER PICTURE. Find out how many of each item your partner has, and record the number in the spaces provided.

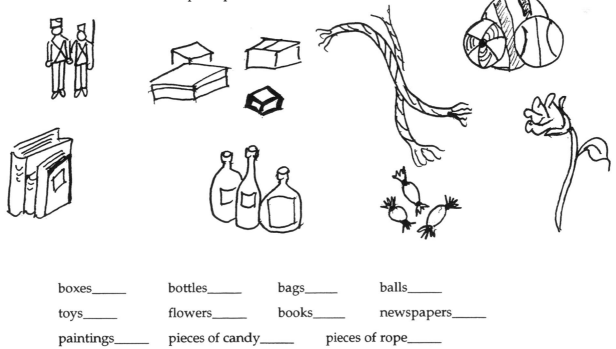

boxes_____   bottles_____   bags_____   balls_____

toys_____   flowers_____   books_____   newspapers_____

paintings_____   pieces of candy_____   pieces of rope_____

Unit 5c: Rummage sale (A)

You go to a rummage sale. The first set of items below are what you have for sale, each marked with a price. The second set are items you wish to buy. Check among the people in your group to see what is available at what price. Write in the lowest price you can find in the space below each item you will buy. You are not expected to haggle at this sale, and not all items are available.

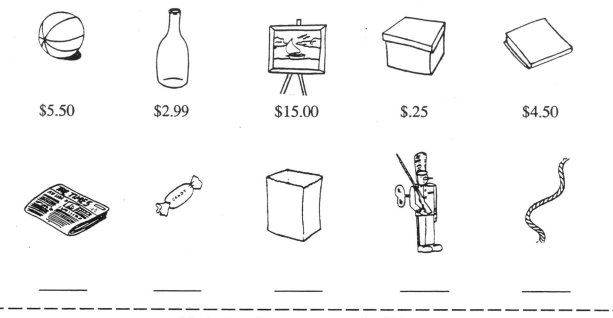

| $5.50 | $2.99 | $15.00 | $.25 | $4.50 |

_____   _____   _____   _____   _____

- -

Unit 5c: Rummage sale (B)

You go to a rummage sale. The first set of items below are what you have for sale, each marked with a price. The second set are items you wish to buy. Check among the people in your group to see what is available at what price. Write in the lowest price you can find in the space below each item you will buy. You are not expected to haggle at this sale, and not all items are available.

| $7.20 | $12.89 | $3.50 | $.20 | $5.45 |

_____   _____   _____   _____   _____

Unit 5c: Rummage sale (C)

You go to a rummage sale. The first set of items below are what you have for sale, each marked with a price. The second set are items you wish to buy. Check among the people in your group to see what is available at what price. Write in the lowest price you can find in the space below each item you will buy. You are not expected to haggle at this sale, and not all items are available.

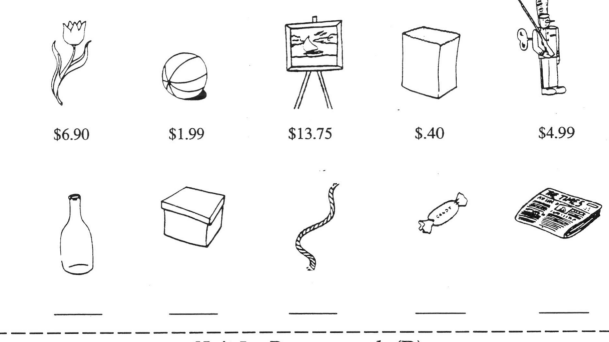

| $6.90 | $1.99 | $13.75 | $.40 | $4.99 |

Unit 5c: Rummage sale (D)

You go to a rummage sale. The first set of items below are what you have for sale, each marked with a price. The second set are items you wish to buy. Check among the people in your group to see what is available at what price. Write in the lowest price you can find in the space below each item you will buy. You are not expected to haggle at this sale, and not all items are available.

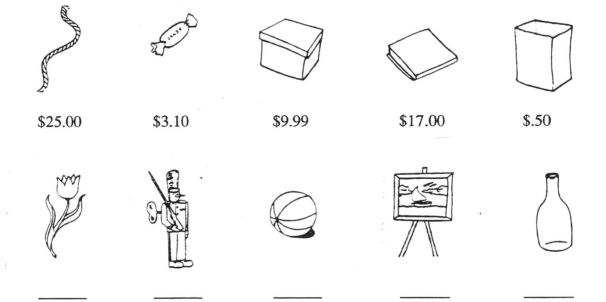

| $25.00 | $3.10 | $9.99 | $17.00 | $.50 |

Unit 5d

Materials required
• Reprints of the masters provided.

• Unit pictures.

Introduction
• Introduce materials using Guessing and the instructor's set of picture-cards or, wherever possible, the clothing of individual students in the class.

Comprehension Drills
• Use Guessing.

• Drill by naming items of clothing that your students are wearing, and having students who are wearing those items raise their hands. (Shei chuan kafei se de duanku? You yige ren chuan hong chenshan. You yige ren chuan huise de qunzi. Shei chuan bai maoyi?)

• Brainstorm for variations of the sample statements and questions provided.

Oral Practice
• Using Inner/outer circles, have the students try to name every item of clothing his/her partner is wearing, adding descriptive elements whenever possible (yijian hong maoyi).

• Play a classroom variation of the Chinese game Dafeng chui. The variation, Zhao ren "Looking for someone", proceeds as follows.

The students arrange their seats in a large circle, leaving enough space between seats to allow easy access. The teacher stands in the middle of the circle and, as the first "caller," begins the following chant.

> Caller: "Wo zai zhao yige ren." (I am looking for someone.)
>
> Class (together): "Ni zhao shei?" (Who are you looking for?)
>
> Caller: "Wo zhao chuan ...de ren." (I am looking for someone wearing ...)

Any item of clothing can fit the blank in the last line: red shirts, shorts, white shoes, etc.

As soon as the caller has said that last line, (for instance, "Wo zhao chuan bai xiezi de ren") anyone who fits the description (anyone wearing white shoes) must get up and swap seats with someone else fitting the same description. The teacher quickly grabs a seat as soon as someone leaves it. Thus, when the dust has settled, one person will again be left standing in the center. This person is the new caller, and the procedure begins again. Continue as time allows (say, 15 minutes).

• Have the students listen to the audiotape and complete the Dialog Practice exercise for homework. Check in class.

• Break the class into groups of 3 to rehearse "Wash-day." Have one group perform for the class.

Controlled use
• Divide the students into groups of 3 or 4. Distribute forms A-D of "Clothing Sale," one set to each group, and have them complete the task assigned. When all groups are done, check together for the lowest available price of all items.

Unit 5d: Clothing sale (A)

You go to a clothing sale. The first set of clothing items below are what you have for sale, each marked with a price. The second set are items you wish to buy. Check among the people in your group to see what is available at what price. Write in the lowest price you can find in the space below each item you will buy. You are not expected to haggle at this sale.

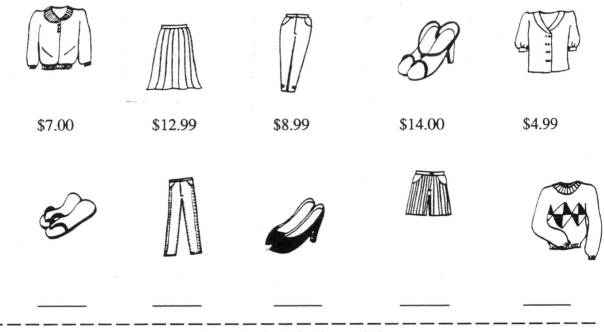

| $7.00 | $12.99 | $8.99 | $14.00 | $4.99 |

_____   _____   _____   _____   _____

- -

Unit 5d: Clothing (B)

You go to a clothing sale. The first set of clothing items below are what you have for sale, each marked with a price. The second set are items you wish to buy. Check among the people in your group to see what is available at what price. Write in the lowest price you can find in the space below each item you will buy. You are not expected to haggle at this sale.

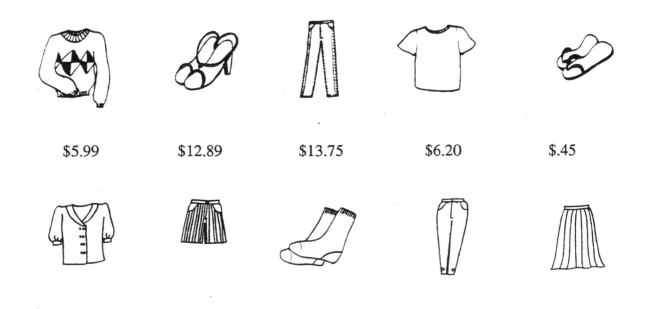

| $5.99 | $12.89 | $13.75 | $6.20 | $.45 |

_____   _____   _____   _____   _____

Unit 5d: Clothing sale (C)

You go to a clothing sale. The first set of clothing items below are what you have for sale, each marked with a price. The second set are items you wish to buy. Check among the people in your group to see what is available at what price. Write in the lowest price you can find in the space below each item you will buy. You are not expected to haggle at this sale.

$2.22 $7.45 $13.00 $4.40 $3.75

_____   _____   _____   _____   _____

- -

Unit 5d: Clothing sale (D)

You go to a clothing sale. The first set of clothing items below are what you have for sale, each marked with a price. The second set are items you wish to buy. Check among the people in your group to see what is available at what price. Write in the lowest price you can find in the space below each item you will buy. You are not expected to haggle at this sale.

$6.25 $3.95 $9.99 $39.00 $5.50

_____   _____   _____   _____   _____

Unit 5e

Materials required

•Buyers' and Sellers' bags, assembled as follows.

Materials:

Twenty-eight brown paper bags.

A total of 80 "filler" items, as follows:

Two photocopies of the "Painting" handout attached. Cut the copies apart on the broken lines, for a total of 10 slips.

Two photocopies of the "Toy" handout attached. Cut the copies apart on the broken lines, for a total of 10 slips.

Three yards of ribbon, cut as follows: 2 segments 4" long, 2 segments 7" long, 2 segments 10" long, 2 segments 13" long, and 2 segments 16" long; total of 10 segments.

Five swatches of cloth of different weights (some thicker, some thinner) but preferably all in the same color. Cut each swatch in half; total: 10 swatches.

Five different grades of sandpaper, varying from coarse to fine. Cut each piece in half. Total: 10 pieces.

One-foot lengths of string in 5 different thicknesses. (The only difference between each item should be the thickness of it, not the color or the material.) Cut each length in half; total: 10 lengths.

Two identical sets of 5 pellets. Each of the 5 should be of a perceptibly different weight. Total: 10 pellets.

Two identical sets of 5 plastic or silk flowers, ranging in shade from dark to light (10 flowers in all, 2 of each shade). Total: 10 flowers.

Procedure:

Assemble 1 set of 8 bags for the sellers. Fill these as follows

> Bag 1: 1 photocopied set of the "Painting" handout, cut apart on the broken lines.
>
> Bag 2: 1 photocopied set of the "Toy" handout, cut apart on the broken lines.
>
> Bag 3: 1 set of the 5 different lengths of ribbon.
>
> Bag 4: 1 set of the 5 different weights of cloth.
>
> Bag 5: 1 set of the 5 different grades of sandpaper.
>
> Bag 6: 1 set of the 5 different thicknesses of twine, string, or chain.
>
> Bag 7: 1 set of the 5 different weights of bullets or pellets.
>
> Bag 8: 1 set of the 5 different shades of flowers.

Label each bag by content, using the following list: huà, wánjù, căidài, bù, shāzhǐ, shéngzi, xiǎo tánwán, huā.

Divide the remaining 20 bags you have prepared into 2 sets of 10 bags each: label each bag in one set "Buyer's set 1" and each bag in the second set "Buyer's set 2." Fill the bags in "Buyer's set 1" with 4 items selected at random from the remaining 40 "filler" items you have prepared. Do not put more than 1 type of thing in each bag (don't select 2 grades of sandpaper for the same bag, for instance). Write on the outside of each bag a listing of the contents, i.e. 4 of the following on each bag: yì zhāng huàr, yíge wánjù, yìtiáo căidài, yíkuài bù, yíkuài shāzhǐ, yìtiáo shéngzi, yìkē xiǎo tánwán, yìduǒ huār. The bags in "Buyer's set 2" remain empty.

•Reprints of the masters provided.

Introduction
•Use Pantomime to introduce the vocabulary in this lesson.

Comprehension Drills
•Use Pantomime.

Oral Practice

•Form the students into pairs. Distribute one copy of "Which?" to each student, and have them complete the task assigned.

•Have the students listen to the audiotape and complete the Dialog Practice exercise for homework. Check in class.

•Break the class into pairs to rehearse "Getting Dressed." Have one group perform for the class.

•Brainstorm for variations of the sample statements and questions provided on the vocabulary sheet.

Controlled use

•Play "Picky-picky" as follows. Divide your class into three groups: buyers, sellers, and runners. Assign eight students to be sellers, assign up to ten students to be buyers and have the rest be runners (there should be at least five runners). If these numbers do not match your class, adjust as necessary; there should be approximately balanced numbers of buyers, sellers, and runners.

Have the buyers sit side-by-side in one row and the sellers sit side-by-side in another row, at two opposite ends of the classroom. The buyers face the wall, and the sellers face the center of the classroom and the backs of the buyers. The runners move around in the space in the middle, lined up approximately one per buyer.

The sellers each get one of the set of seller's bags. The buyers each get 2 bags: one filled one from "Buyer's set 1," which they place in front of them, and one empty one from "Buyer's set 2" which they place beside them.

Either tape a copy of "Picky-picky: TERMINOLOGY" to the board, or photocopy it onto a transparency and project it using an overhead projector.

Photocopy copies of "Picky-picky (Buyer/Seller/Runner)" and cut them apart on the broken lines. Hand out the appropriate intructions to each student, and go over them together. (You may even wish to take the place of a buyer and do a demonstration transaction). Then allow them to get started. After all the buyers have found matches for all the items in their bags, this round is over. Remember to ask the buyers to transfer all items from "Buyer's set 2" back into "Buyer's set 1," in preparation for the next round. Ideally, you will be able to rotate the students so that each of them gets a chance to play each of the three roles.

Unit 5e: Which?

Circle one selection from each set below, at random. Your partner will do the same. Your task is to interview your partner to decide which one he/she has selected, and he/she will try to find out the same from you.

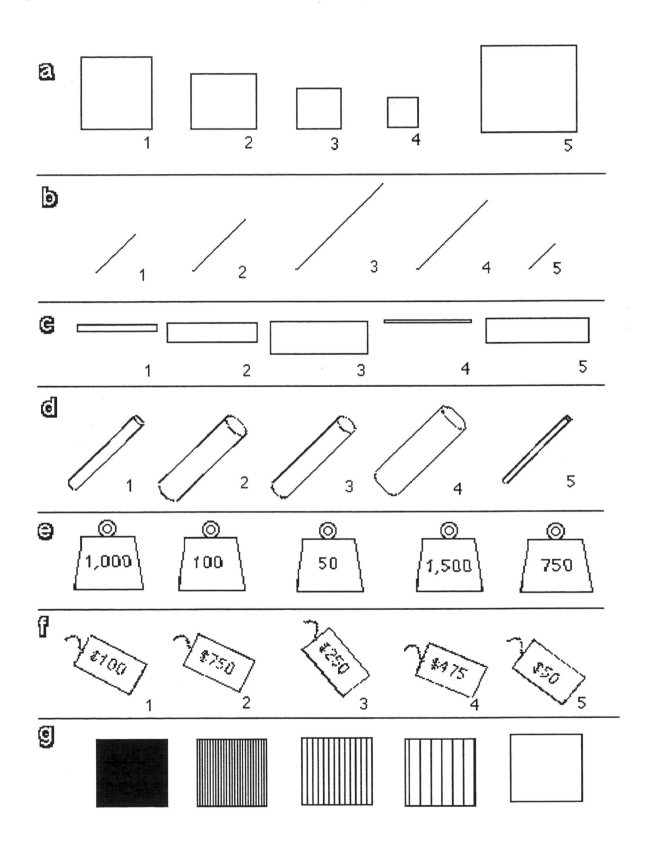

Unit 5e: Picky-picky (Buyer)

You have a buyer's bag with some items in it. Take these items out and look at them, and then put them back in the bag. DO NOT LET YOUR RUNNER SEE THEM. The names of these objects are written on the bag.

Pretend that you will at some point in the (distant) future need to order large quantities of the items in your bag; your task in this activity is to find out if the sellers (behind you) have available exactly what you want, in the right length, shade, weight, grain, etc.

Your runner is waiting to assist you. Work on your items one at a time. Pick one item. Let's suppose it is a ribbon. Inform your runner, "Wo yào mai caidài." Your runner will go and hunt among the sellers until he/she finds a ribbon to bring back to you. Compare it with your ribbon. It will likely be either too long or too short. Let's say it is too long. Send it back to the seller, and say, "Wo yào duan yìdiar de." YOU MAY NOT SHOW ANYTHING TO YOUR RUNNER. He/she will go back to the sellers and bring back a shorter ribbon (you hope). Continue until you have made an exact match. Raise your hand, show the pair of items to your instructor, and if your instructor agrees they match, put one into the empty bag beside you, and send the other back to the seller via your runner.

Repeat for each of the other items in your buyer's bag. You have completed your task when you have transferred all the items from one bag into the other.

Unit 5e: Picky-picky (Seller)

You have a bag full of goods, clearly labeled on the outside. Turn your bag so that the label faces you, check out its contents, but DON'T SHOW THE CONTENTS OF YOUR BAG (OR ITS LABEL) TO ANYONE ELSE.

The buyers sitting on the other side of the room from you will want to know if your goods are what they want, and will be somewhat picky. They will communicate with you through a runner. The runners will first come to ask what you are selling. Supposing you are selling ribbons. Say "Wo mài caidài." Eventually one or more of the runners will come to you and ask for a ribbon. Send one at random, and wait for a response. If the runner returns and asks for a slightly different one ("Wo yào duan yìdiar de"), select an appropriate ribbon in response and exchange it with the one the runner has brought back. If the ribbon that your current runner is requesting is being "checked out" by another seller, ask the runner to wait: "Qing deng yìhúir." Continue until the teacher tells you this round over.

Unit 5e: Picky-picky (Runner)

Your job in this activity is to transmit messages and items between the buyer and seller. DO NOT LOOK AT ANY OF THE ITEMS THE BUYER AND SELLER HAVE IN THEIR POSSESSION, until one is handed to you.

Begin with the buyer. He/she will tell you what to look for—say, a ribbon. Go to the sellers and ask each in turn, "Ni mài caidài ma?" until you find one who sells ribbons. That seller will give you a ribbon to carry back to your buyer. Hand it to your buyer and say "Na (here)." He/she may find something wrong with it: "Tài cháng le. Wo yào duan yìdiar de." Take the ribbon back to the seller and say, "Wo yào duan yìdiar de." Exchange your ribbon for the new one the seller will give you, and carry it back to the buyer. Continue this process until the teacher tells you the round is over.

118

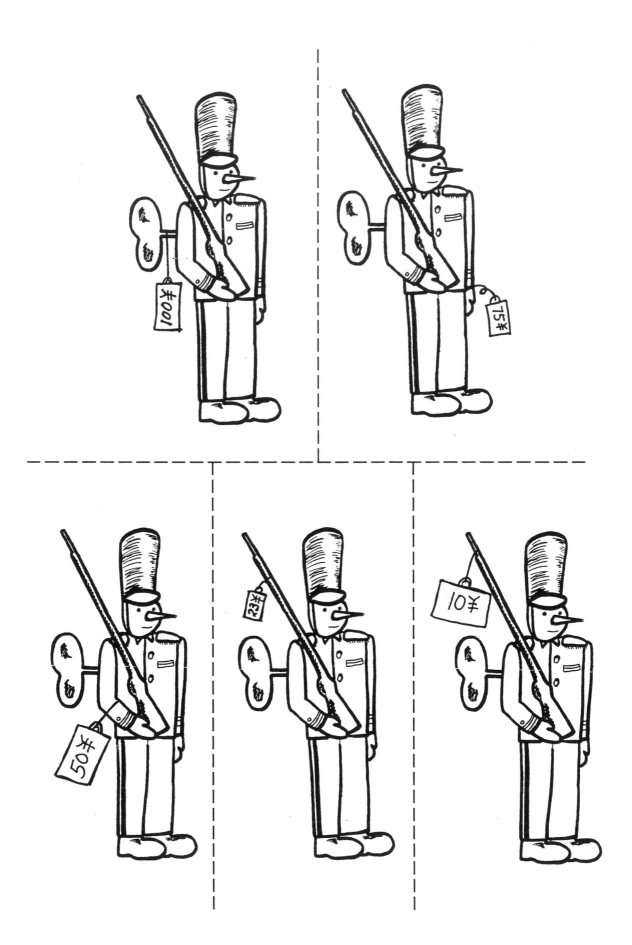

Unit 5e: Picky-picky (TERMINOLOGY)

huàr: dà / xiǎo

wánjù: guì / piányí

cǎidài: cháng / duǎn

bù: hòu / báo

shāzhǐ: cū / xì

shéngzǐ: cū / xì

tánwán: zhòng / qīng

huàr: yánsè qīng/ yánsè qiǎn

Unit 6a

Materials required

•Color-cards; one instructor's set and one set for each of your students. If these are not available commercially, construct them as follows.

<u>Materials:</u> Several sheets of construction or artist's colored paper in each of the necessary colors. Scissors, hole punch; access to a laminating machine. Key rings (.75" or 1" in diameter; available at drug stores); one for each set of color cards.

<u>Procedure:</u> Cut the paper to make one card for the instructor (say 25 sq" in area) and one card for each of your students (each say 10 sq" in area) in each color. Laminate the cards to protect them. Punch a hole in one corner of each card. Separate the cards into sets containing one card of each color and secure each set with a key ring.

•Several sets of color crayons or pens; several pairs of scissors.

•Reprints of the masters provided.

Introduction

•Use Guessing and the instructor's set of color-cards.

Comprehension Drills

•Use Picture-card drills, substituting the students' individual sets of color-cards.

Oral Practice

•Using Inner/outer circles, have the students try to name colors that appear on their partner's clothing, adding the name of the item whenever possible (<u>Ni zher you kafeise, hui se, gen fenhong se. Ni de xiezi shi hei se de. Zheige shi lanse de</u>. etc.).

•Play <u>Zhao ren</u> "Looking for someone" (see the <u>Practice</u> section of Unit 5d), using color terms as much as possible in the chant. (<u>Wo zhao chuan fenhong se de chenshan de ren</u>.)

•Have the students listen to the audiotape and complete the Dialog Practice exercise for homework. Check in class.

•Divide the class into groups of 5 to rehearse "A Poster." Have 1-2 groups perform.

•Brainstorm for variations of the sample statements and questions provided.

Controlled use

•Divide your class into small groups of 3-4 students each. Number the groups. Give each group one copy of "Ah Mao and Xiao Fang," loan them a set of the color pens and a pair of scissors, and ask each group to complete the task assigned. They do this by consensus: one person wields the pens and the others tell him/her what color to make each item of clothing (<u>Ba ta chenshan tu huangse; ba ta xiezi tu hongse</u>). When they are done, collect all the pictures from them.

•Separate the Ah Mao and Xiao Fang pictures, and shuffle each set. Tape up the Ah Mao pictures at random on one side of the blackboard, and the Xiao Fang pictures on the opposite side. The students now need to reunite each couple as created by the student who colored them: Ah Mao by Group 1 with Xiao Fang by Group 1, Ah Mao by Group 2 with Xiao Fang by Group 2, etc. To this end, ask members of one group to describe their first their Ah Mao, then their Xiao Fang, and then ask a volunteer to point out the two people described, but leave the figures in their taped positions. Continue for each of the other groups. When all the figures have been identified, ask for volunteers to come to the blackboard and take down matching pairs of figures, describing each as he/she does so. If problems arise, have the original groups re-describe the figures to help with identification.

Unit 6a: Ah Máo and Xiǎo Fāng

These two people (Ah Mao is the male and Xiao Fang is the female) have been on a shopping spree, and are trying on all their purchases. Their clothes don't actually go together very well. Color their clothing as you wish, making sure that you use most if not all of the colors listed.

red blue green yellow orange pink brown purple black white grey gold silver

Then cut this piece of paper in half lengthwise, so that Ah Mao and Xiao Fang are separated. Write the number of your group lightly in pencil on the back of each half paper.

Unit 6b

Materials required

• Reprints of the masters provided.

• Unit pictures.

Introduction

• Use Pantomime.

Comprehension Drills

• Use either Pantomime or Guessing, or some combination of both.

Oral Practice

• Have your students form pairs. Distribute a copy of "Finding a Friend" to each student, and have them complete the task assigned. As a follow-up activity, as for volunteers to describe their partner's "day" to the class.

• Have the students listen to the audiotape and complete the Dialog Practice exercise for homework. Check in class.

• Divide the class into groups of 5 to rehearse "After the Poster." Have 1-2 groups perform.

• Brainstorm for variations of the sample statements and questions provided on the vocabulary sheet.

Controlled use

• Form your class into small groups of four to five people each. Photocopy and cut apart "Finding something to do," and distribute it by group so that each student has a slip. Groups with five students will have all five slips, A-E, one per student. For groups with only four students, leave out slip E. Have them converse with each other to complete the task assigned.

Correct answer: play cards

• If there is time to repeat the exercise, use the slips entitled "Finding something else to do."

Correct answer: listen to music

Unit 6b: Finding a Friend

Look at the list of activities below, and check off the four that most interest you. Next, interview as many of your classmates as you can in the time allotted, to see which of them might have the same interests you do. Ask of each "Ni xihuan zuo shenme?"

	You	*Partner 1*	*Partner 2*	*Partner 3*	*Partner 4*
Reading					
Watching TV					
Watching movies					
Listening to music					
Writing letters					
Walking					
Window-shopping					
Shopping					
Talking on phone					
Playing ball					
Playing cards					
Swimming					

Name of classmate whose tastes are closest to yours:

Unit 6b: Finding something to do (A)

It is a Saturday. You and your friends are bored. You would like to do something (anything!) together with them, but you hate reading, listening to music, and going for walks. Anything else would be fine. Find something you can do together.

- -

Unit 6b: Finding something to do (B)

It is a Saturday. You and your friends are bored. You would like to do something (anything!) together with them, but you hate watching TV, talking on the telephone, and window-shopping. Anything else would be fine. Find something you can do together.

- -

Unit 6b: Finding something to do (C)

It is a Saturday. You and your friends are bored. You would like to do something (anything!) together with them, but you hate movies, playing ball, and going shopping. Anything else would be fine. Find something you can do together.

- -

Unit 6b: Finding something to do (D)

It is a Saturday. You and your friends are bored. You would like to do something (anything!) together with them, but you hate listening to music, writing letters, and swimming. Anything else would be fine. Find something you can do together.

- -

Unit 6b: Finding something to do (E)

It is a Saturday. You and your friends are bored. You would like to do something (anything!) together with them, but you hate writing letters, playing ball and swimming. Anything else would be fine. Find something you can do together.

■ ■

Unit 6b: Finding something else to do (A)

Now it is Sunday afternoon. You and your friends are bored. You would like to do something (anything!) together with them, but you hate playing cards, writing letters, and swimming. Anything else would be fine. Find something you can do together.

- -

Unit 6b: Finding something else to do (B)

Now it is Sunday afternoon. You and your friends are bored. You would like to do something (anything!) together with them, but you hate reading, talking on the telephone, and going shopping. Anything else would be fine. Find something you can do together.

- -

Unit 6b: Finding something else to do (C)

Now it is Sunday afternoon. You and your friends are bored. You would like to do something (anything!) together with them, but you hate window-shopping, playing any kind of ball, and watching television. Anything else would be fine. Find something you can do together.

- -

Unit 6b: Finding something else to do (D)

Now it is Sunday afternoon. You and your friends are bored. You would like to do something (anything!) together with them, but you hate movies, writing letters, and going for walks. Anything else would be fine. Find something you can do together.

- -

Unit 6b: Finding something else to do (E)

Now it is Sunday afternoon. You and your friends are bored. You would like to do something (anything!) together with them, but you hate talking on the telephone, going to the movies, and playing any kind of ball. Anything else would be fine. Find something you can do together.

Unit 7a

Materials required

•Four blank index cards, 5" x 8" or larger. Write "North," "South," "East," and "West" in large, dark letters on the cards.

•Masking tape.

•A stuffed panda, or any other kind of animal (optional).

•Several sheets of construction or artists' paper, in each of the following colors: red, white, blue, green, brown, black.

•One letter-sized envelope for each student in your class.

•Reprints of the masters provided.

Introduction

•Using masking tape, delineate a square on the floor. Designate one side of the square as north, and then tape "North," "South," "East," and "West" into appropriate positions on the floor, outside of the box. Introduce <u>dongbiar</u>, <u>nanbiar</u>, <u>xibiar</u>, <u>beibiar</u>, and <u>zhongjiar</u> to the students by walking from location to location in and around the box, saying "<u>Wo zai zhongjiar</u>," "<u>Wo zai beibiar</u>," "<u>Wo zai nanbiar</u>," etc. If you find a volunteer to move around for you, you could say "<u>Maria zai xibiar</u>," "<u>Maria zai zhongjiar</u>," etc. Remove the cards and demonstrate <u>litóu</u> and <u>wàitóu</u> by stepping in and out of the square.

•Stand inside the square, and make handmotions first for someone to join you, and then for the person to leave. As the volunteer performs these motions, introduce <u>jinlai</u> and <u>chuqu</u>.

•Place a chair inside the square and have a volunteer sit on it. Introduce the panda ("<u>Zhe shi Xiao Xiongmao</u>"), and then use the panda to introduce the relative positions "in front," "behind," "on top," "below," "on the left," and "on the right." ("<u>Xiao Xiongmao zai ni qiantou</u>," "<u>Xiao Xiongmao zai ni shangtou</u>," "<u>Xiao Xiongmao zai ni zuobiar</u>," etc.)

Comprehension Drills

•Individual or groups of students move in and around the box in accordance to cues given by the teacher. ("<u>Ni zai beibiar</u>," "<u>Ni zai zhongjiar</u>," "<u>Ni zai litou</u>." "<u>Jinlai!</u>" "<u>Chuqu!</u>" etc.)

•Have the students each hold something in their hands to take the place of <u>Xiao Xiongmao</u>. (You could take the red cards from the color cards used in unit 6a, pass them out, and introduce them as <u>Xiao Hong</u>.) Have them hold the item in the appropriate location relative to themselves, according to your cues. ("<u>Xiao Hong zai ni youbiar</u>," "<u>Xiao Hong zai ni qiantou</u>," etc.)

Oral Practice

•Cut up the colored paper into rectangles approximately .5" x .25", so that each student has two rectangles in each color. Separate the pieces into sets—one set per student—and store each set separately in an envelope. Distribute one set to each student. Have them form pairs. Distribute "Color Play," one per student, and have them complete the tasks assigned.

•Have the students listen to the audiotape and complete the Dialog Practice exercise at home. Check in class.

•Divide the class into groups of 4 to rehearse "Visiting Zhang." Have one group perform.

•Brainstorm for variations of the sample statements and questions provided.

Controlled use

•Have the students form pairs. Distribute one copy of "Where is everyone? (Your answers)" and one copy of "Where is everyone? (Your partner's answers)" to EACH student, so that they all have two sheets of paper apiece, and have them complete the task assigned.

Unit 7a: Color play (A)

The colors named in the first circle below correspond to the slips of colored paper you have received. Give your partner precise descriptions of the location of each "slip," so that s/he can duplicate your patterns on the blank circle provided on his/her sheet of paper. Eg: <u>Yǒu liǎngge lánde. Yíge zài běibiār, yíge zài dōngbiar...</u>

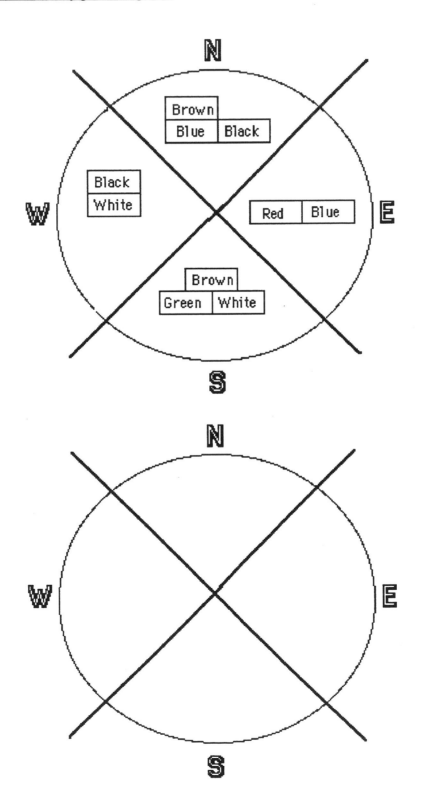

Unit 7a: Color play (B)

The colors named in the second circle below correspond to the slips of colored paper you have received. Give your partner precise descriptions of the location of each "slip," so that s/he can duplicate your patterns on the blank circle provided on his/her sheet of paper. Eg: <u>Yǒu liǎngge lánde. Yíge zài běibiār, yíge zài dōngbiar...</u>

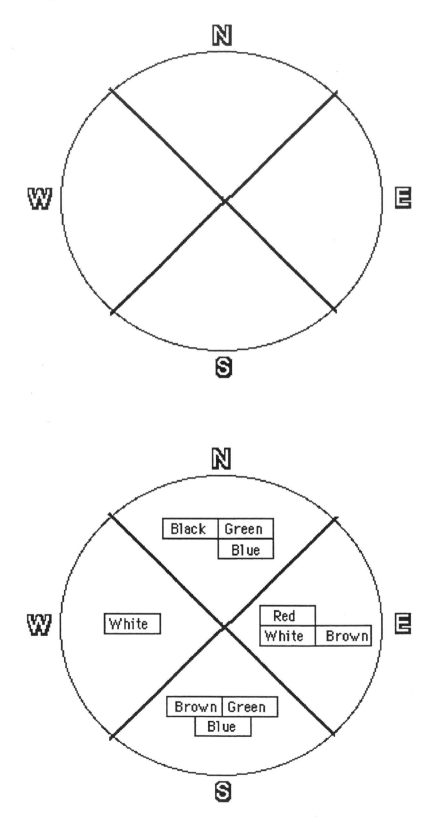

Unit 7a: Where is everyone? (Your answers)

Decide the whereabouts of each of the following people by writing a number from the list below in the rectangles (representing houses) in part I, and in the circles (representing people's heads) in parts II-IV.

1) *Xiǎo Wáng*   2) *Láo Lǐ*   3) *Zhāng Nǚshì*   4) *Zhào Xiānsheng*   5) *Liú Yīsheng*   6) *Lín Xiáojie*
7) *Jiǎng Tàitai*   8) *Sūn Lùshī*   9) *Chén Lǎoshī*   10) *Féng Huìwēi*   11) *Péng Dàilì*   12) *Dù Rénfù*

I. Where do they live?

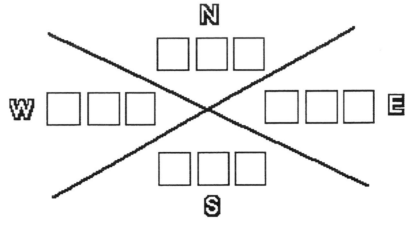

II. Is everyone inside the house?

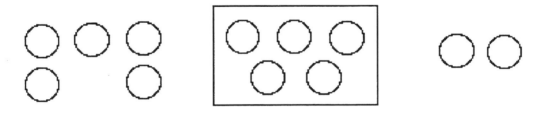

III. Where is everyone standing?

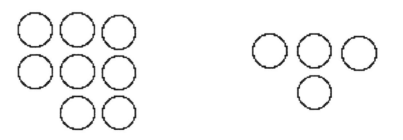

IV. Are they coming in or going out?

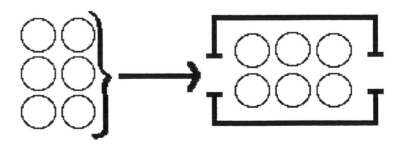

Unit 7a: Where is everyone? (Your partner's answers)

Find out what your partner has decided for people's locations. Write numbers to match what your partner has written, in each rectangle and circle below. Sample questions are given for each part.

1) Xiǎo Wáng   2) Láo Lǐ   3) Zhāng Nǚshì   4) Zhào Xiānsheng   5) Liú Yīsheng   6) Lín Xiáojie
7) Jiǎng Tàitai   8) Sūn Lùshī   9) Chén Lǎoshī   10) Féng Huìwēi   11) Péng Dàilì   12) Dù Rénfū

I. Where do they live? (Xiǎo Wáng zhù zài nǎr? Láo Lǐ ne? Shéi zhù zài běibiār? Háiyǒu shéi zhù zài běibiār? Xībiār ne?)

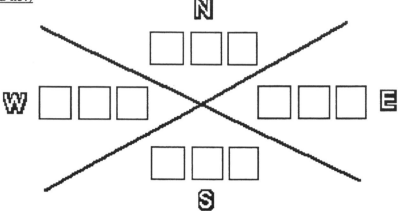

II. Is everyone in the house? (Shéi zài lǐtóu? Shéi zài wàitóu? Chén Lǎoshī zài nǎr?)

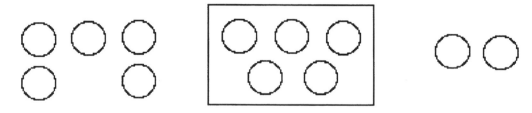

III. Where is everyone standing? (Shéi zài zuǒbiār? Shéi zài qiántóu? Dù Rénfū zài nǎr?)

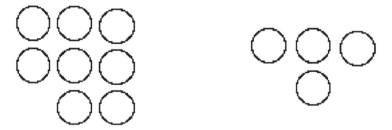

IV. Are they coming in or going out? (Shéi jìnlái? Shéi chūqù?)

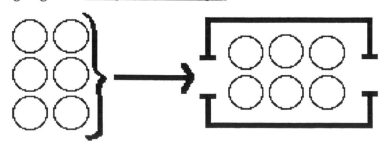

Unit 7b

Materials required
• Reprints of the masters provided.

• Unit pictures.

Introduction
• Use the unit pictures. To make your introduction more effective, draw the outline of a house and the floorplans for various floors on the blackboard, and point to various locations or place the pictures in various locations as you describe them.

Comprehension Drills
• Use Picture-card drills.

Oral Practice
• Have your students form pairs. Distribute one copy of "This is my house" to each student, and have them complete the task assigned.

• Have the students listen to the audiotape and complete the Dialog Practice exercise for homework. Check in class.

• Divide the class into groups of 4 to rehearse "Privacy." Have one group perform.

• Brainstorm for variations of the sample statements and questions provided on the vocabulary sheet.

Controlled use
For homework, each student draws the layout of a house in which they have lived or are living, labelling each room in English. (Have them use a black pen.) The student's name is written lightly in pencil on the back of the paper. Collect the layouts and make one photocopy of each. The student's name does not appear on the photocopy.

• Distribute one photocopied layout to each student, ensuring that no-one gets their own. The students form pairs or groups of three, and describe the layout they have received to each other. Each group then selects one layout, and together rehearse a description of it, taking turns describing different aspects. Find the original of each of the layouts the different groups will describe, tape these to the blackboard in random order, and label them with numbers or letters (written in chalk under or above the picture). Groups then take turns making presentations. After each presentation, let all the students approach, examine the layouts on the blackboard, and decide (either privately or jointly) which layout was just described.

• For a follow-up activity, collect all layouts again, shuffle, and redistribute to individual students. Volunteers take turns describing the layouts they have received. At the end of each description, the student who "belongs" to that house identifies him/herself and reclaims the layout.

Unit 7b: This is my house

Decide whether you are "A" and your partner "B," or vice versa. Below are two floorplans for a Sinified home. Using the symbols given, decide what each of the rooms is in your home. Draw a symbol in each of the rooms in A if you are A, B if you are B. Then exchange information with your partner to find out each other's floorplan. Ask questions such as <u>Wòfáng zài nâr?</u> and <u>Chúfáng hòubiär shì shénme?</u>

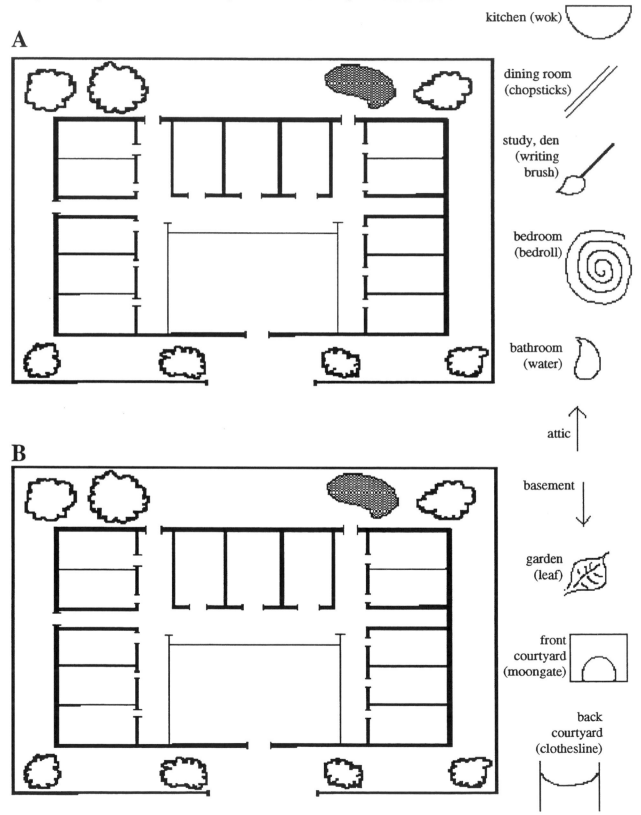

kitchen (wok)

dining room (chopsticks)

study, den (writing brush)

bedroom (bedroll)

bathroom (water)

attic

basement

garden (leaf)

front courtyard (moongate)

back courtyard (clothesline)

Unit 7c

Materials required
•Reprints of the masters provided.

•Unit pictures.

Introduction
•Use Guesswork and the unit pictures.

Comprehension Drills
•Use Picture-card drills.

Oral Practice
•The students form pairs. Each receives a copy of "This is my room," and completes the task assigned.

•Have the students listen to the audiotape and complete the Dialog Practice exercise for homework. Check in class.

•Divide the class into pairs to rehearse "Remembering Zhang's Room." Have 1-2 groups perform for the class.

•Brainstorm for variations of the sample statements and questions provided on the vocabulary sheet.

Controlled use
For homework, each student draws the layout of their room, labelling each item in English. The student's name is written lightly in pencil on the back of the paper. Collect the layouts and make one photocopy of each. The student's name does not appear on the photocopy.

•Distribute one photocopied layout to each student, ensuring that no-one gets their own. The students form pairs or groups of three, and describe the layout they have received to each other. Each group then selects one layout, and together rehearse a description of it, taking turns describing different aspects. Find the original of each of the layouts the different groups will describe, tape these to the blackboard in random order, and label them with numbers or letters (written in chalk under or above the picture). Groups then take turns making presentations. After each presentation, let all the students approach, examine the layouts on the blackboard, and decide (either privately or jointly) which layout was just described.

•For a follow-up activity, collect all layouts again, shuffle, and redistribute to individual students. Volunteers take turns describing the layouts they have received. At the end of each description, the student who "belongs" to that room identifies him/herself and reclaims the layout.

Unit 7c: This is my room

Decide whether you are "A" and your partner "B," or vice versa.

Below are two outlines of a room. Decide what furniture is in your room, and indicate the location of the furniture, using the symbols given. Draw the symbols in room A if you are A, B if you are B. Then exchange information with your partner to find out the arrangement of each other's room. Ask questions such as Nǐde fángjiān lǐtóu yǒu shūzhuō ma? and Chuáng zài nǎr?

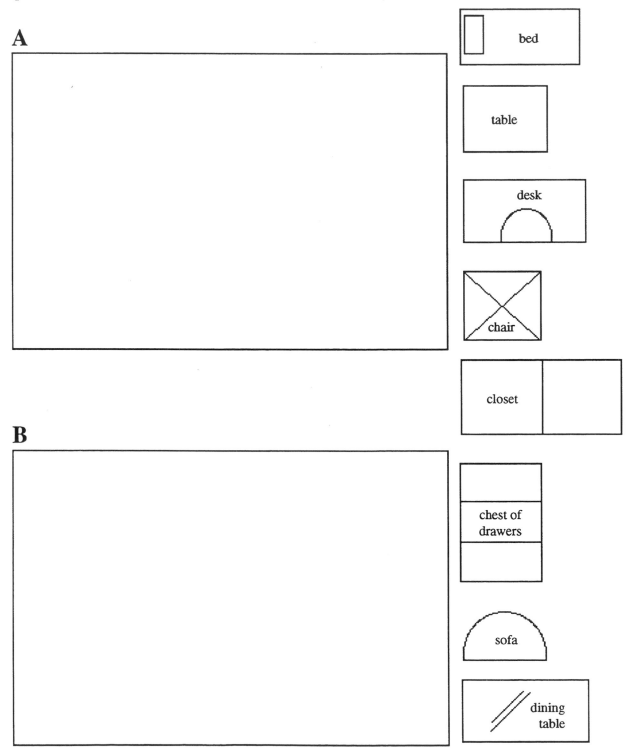

Unit 7d

Materials required
• Reprints of the masters provided.

• Unit pictures.

Introduction
• Use Pantomime, and/or the unit pictures.

Comprehension Drills
• Use Pantomime and/or Picture-card drills.

Oral Practice
• The students form pairs. Each receives a copy of "This is my day," and completes the task assigned.

• Have the students listen to the audiotape and complete the Dialog Practice exercise for homework. Check in class.

• Divide the class into pairs to rehearse "Morning Routines." Have 1-2 groups perform.

• Brainstorm for variations of the sample statements and questions provided on the vocabulary sheet.

Controlled use
• The activity "What time is it?" can be conducted in pairs, between small groups, or as a whole class activity. Instructions here are for a whole class exercise.

Each student receives a copy of "What time is it?" The teacher (or a student volunteer), as IT, secretly selects a time. This becomes the time it is "now;" everyone else has to guess what time it is "now." To do this, they take turns asking questions about what IT has or hasn't done so far. Examples:

Student 1:	Nǐ shuā yá le ma?	IT: Hái méi.
Student 2:	Nǐ xǐliǎn le ma?	IT: Xǐ le.
Student 3:	Nǐ xǐzǎo le ma?	IT: Zhèng zài xǐ ne.
	Xiànzài bādiǎn zhōng ma?	IT: Duì, bādiǎn zhōng.

Student 3 then takes a turn as IT.

Unit 7d: *This is my day*

Write IN ENGLISH what you do every day, and the approximate time you do it. Use the column on the left.
Then ask your partner questions about his/her daily activities, and fill in the column on the right, also in English.

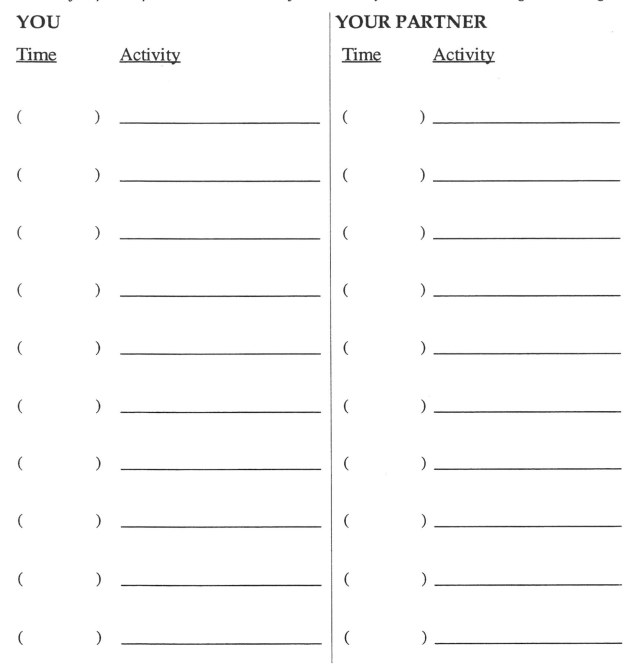

YOU		YOUR PARTNER	
Time	Activity	Time	Activity
( )	_____	( )	_____
( )	_____	( )	_____
( )	_____	( )	_____
( )	_____	( )	_____
( )	_____	( )	_____
( )	_____	( )	_____
( )	_____	( )	_____
( )	_____	( )	_____
( )	_____	( )	_____
( )	_____	( )	_____

Suggested Questions:

Nǐ měitiān zuò shénme?

Nǐ xiān zuò shénme?

Ránhòu zuò shénme?

Nǐ měitiān dōu xǐ yīfu ma?

Nǐ jǐ diǎnzhōng xǐ yīfu?

Unit 7d: What time is it?

On the left is "IT's" daily schedule. Chinese equivalents of the activities are on the right, in scrambled order.

6:15	get up	hē kāfēi
6:30	*wash face*	xíliǎn
6:35	brush teeth	huàn yīfu
6:40	**use the toilet**	shàng kè
6:55	drink coffee	dào xuéxiào
7:00	*eat breakfast*	shàng cèsuǒ
7:30	wash dishes	xià kè
8:00	change	hē chá
8:30	leave the house	hē qìshuǐ
8:45	arrive at school	xǐng
9:00	*go to class*	zuò wǎnfàn
10:55	leave class	chī zǎofàn
11:00	go to the library	chī wǎnfàn
12:15	go home	zuò gōngkè
12:20	drink tea	shuì jiào
12:21	use the toilet	shū tóufǎ
12:25	wash hands	dào jiā
12:30	eat lunch	xíwǎn
12:45	drink some soda	xí shǒu
12:50	wash hands	chī wǔfàn
12:52	brush teeth	chūmén
1:00	take a nap	huí jiā
2:00	*wake up*	xízǎo
2:05	wash face	dǎ diànhuà
2:10	leave the house	zhénglǐ fángjiān
2:30	go to class	kàn diànshì
4:25	leave class	kànshū
4:30	go to the library	qù túshūguǎn
5:30	go home	shuì wǔjiào
5:45	arrive home	
6:00	make dinner	
6:30	eat dinner	
6:45	wash dishes	
7:30	make a phone call	
7:40	clean up the room	
7:45	do homework	
9:30	take a bath	
9:50	brush teeth	
9:57	comb hair	
10:00	*watch television*	
10:30	read a book	
11:30	go to sleep	

Unit 8a

Materials required
•Reprints of the masters provided.

•Unit pictures.

Introduction
•Use Guessing with the unit pictures. As an alternative, have the students guess what you are saying by pointing to actual objects in your classroom.

Comprehension Drills
•Use Picture-card drills, or have the students point to actual objects in the classroom.

Oral Practice
•The students form pairs, receive one copy each of "Inventory," and complete the task assigned.

•Have the students listen to the audiotape and complete the Dialog Practice exercise for homework. Check in class.

•Divide the class into pairs to rehearse "Cleaning the Classroom." Have 1-2 groups perform.

•Brainstorm for variations of the sample statements and questions provided on the vocabulary sheet.

Controlled use
•Photocopy enough of the student set of picture cards so that each student can have three items at random from the following list: *pencil sharpeners, globes, maps, posters, electric fans, pencils, ball-point pens, roller pens, rulers, erasers, notebooks, textbooks, dictionaries.* Cut apart the items and distribute.

Photocopy "Mooching," cut apart, and distribute one slip per student. Using either Mingling or Inner-outer circles, have them complete the task assigned. The students begin by asking if their counterpart has the item they need; if so, they request to borrow it. Example:

Student 1: Qingwen, ni you qianbi ma?	*Student 2:* Duibuqi, meiyou.
Student 1: You chizi ma?	*Student 2:* Ye meiyou.
Student 1: You xiangpi ca ma?	*Student 2:* You.
Student 1: Qing ba nide xiangpi ca jie gei wo.	*Student 2:* Hao..na.
Student 1: Xiexie ni, zai jian.	*Student 2:* Ah, qing deng yixia. Ni you haibao ma?

Continue for a predetermined period of time, or until all students are done. Then check together to see what students have borrowed.

Unit 8a: Inventory

I. Think of a classroom OTHER than the one you are currently in.

a. Tell HOW MANY of each of the following items that classroom had.

b. Find out what your partner wrote.

hēibǎn	_____	erasers	_____
bǎncā	_____	pencil sharpeners	_____
zhōng	_____	doors	_____
zìzhǐlǒu	_____	blackboards	_____
xiāobǐjī	_____	clocks	_____
diànfēngshàn	_____	windows	_____
mén	_____	electric fans	_____
chuānghù	_____	wastepaper baskets	_____

Was there airconditioning?

_____ yǒu _____méiyǒu

Was there central heating?

_____ yǒu _____méiyǒu

Was there airconditioning?

_____yǒu _____méiyǒu

Was there central heating?

_____yǒu _____méiyǒu

2a. HOW MANY of the following items items do you have on you now?

2b. Find out the same about your partner.

qiānbǐ	_____	rulers	_____
yuánzibǐ	_____	textbooks	_____
qiānzìbǐ	_____	pencils	_____
chǐzi	_____	dictionaries	_____
xiàngpí cā	_____	ball-point pens	_____
bǐjìběn	_____	roller pens	_____
kèběn	_____	erasers	_____
zìdiǎn	_____	notebooks	_____

Unit 8a: Mooching

Borrow a pencil sharpener, a ruler, and an eraser from one or more of your classmates.

Borrow a pencil, a dictionary, and a map from one or more of your classmates.

Borrow a poster, a ball-point pen, and a notebook from one or more of your classmates.

Borrow a textbook, a globe, and a roller pen from one or more of your classmates.

Borrow an electric fan, a pencil, and a notebook from one or more of your classmates.

Borrow a pencil sharpener, a poster, and an eraser from one or more of your classmates.

Borrow a globe, a ball-point pen, and a ruler from one or more of your classmates.

Borrow a map, a poster, and a textbook from one or more of your classmates.

Borrow an electric fan, a pencil, and a dictionary from one or more of your classmates.

Borrow a roller pen, an electric fan, and a pencil sharpener from one or more of your classmates.

Borrow a textbook, a ball-point pen, and a globe from one or more of your classmates.

Borrow a dictionary, a roller pen, and a map from one or more of your classmates.

Borrow a pencil sharpener, a ruler, and a poster from one or more of your classmates.

Borrow a globe, an eraser, and an electric fan from one or more of your classmates.

Borrow a map, a notebook, and a pencil from one or more of your classmates.

Unit 8b

Materials required

• Academic calendar showing terms and breaks, reproduced on an overhead transparency.

• One student's daily schedule (may be hypothetical), reproduced on an overhead transparency.

• Reprints of the masters provided.

• Unit pictures.

Introduction

• With the academic calendar on the overhead projector, have the students guess at the meaning of what you are saying by responding to questions such as <u>Di yige xueqi jiyue jihao kaishi? Hanjia jiyue jihao kaishi? Di erge xueqi jiyue jihao kaishi?</u>

• With the student's daily schedule on the overhead projector, have the students guess at the meaning of what you are saying by responding to questions such as <u>Xiao Wang</u> (substitute the name of your student model) <u>jidian zhong shang Zhongwen ke? Ta jidian zhong shang dili ke?</u>

Comprehension Drills

• Use Picture-card drills.

Oral Practice

• The students form pairs. One in each pair receives form A and the other receives form B of "Mixed up schedules." They complete the tasks assigned.

• Have the students listen to the audiotape and complete the Dialog Practice exercise for homework. Check in class.

• Divide the class into groups of 3 to rehearse "Plans." Have 1-2 groups perform.

• Brainstorm for variations of the sample statements and questions provided on the vocabulary sheet.

Controlled use

• The students form pairs. Each receives a copy of "That was my year," and completes the task assigned.

Unit 8b: Mixed up schedules. (A)

Your school has accidentally mailed your friend's schedule for the coming semester to you, and yours to your friend. You are now on the telephone to your friend. Find out what you actually are signed up for in each period, and give your friend's schedule to him/her.

Real schedule

8:00	Physics	_____
9:00	Geography	_____
10:00	Literature	_____
11:00	Mathematics	_____
12:00	Lunch	_____
1:00	History	_____
2:00	Chinese	_____

- -

Unit 8b: Mixed up schedules. (B)

Your school has accidentally mailed your friend's schedule for the coming semester to you, and yours to your friend. You are now on the telephone to your friend. Find out what you actually are signed up for in each period, and give your friend's schedule to him/her.

Real schedule

8:00	Chinese	_____
9:00	Biology	_____
10:00	History	_____
11:00	Lunch	_____
12:00	Chemistry	_____
1:00	Mathematics	_____
2:00	Geography	_____

Unit 8b: That was my year.

If you are in secondary school, recall what courses you took last year. If you are past high school, recall what courses you took in your last year of high school.

1a. If you took the following subjects in the 1st semester, write "1"; in the 2nd semester, write "2"; in both semesters, write "1/2." If you didn't take the subject, write "0."

Zhōngwén	_____
wùlǐ	_____
shēngwù	_____
huàxué	_____
shùxué	_____
lìshǐ	_____
dìlǐ	_____
wénxué	_____
tǐyù	_____

1b. Find out the same for your partner.

geography	_____
Chinese	_____
mathematics	_____
literature	_____
physics	_____
physical education	_____
history	_____
chemistry	_____
biology	_____

2a. What did you have in each period?

dìyījié kè	_____
dì'èrjié kè	_____
dìsānjié kè	_____
dísìjié kè	_____
dìwǔjié kè	_____
díliùjié kè	_____

2b. Find out the same for your partner.

first period	_____
second period	_____
third period	_____
fourth period	_____
fifth period	_____
sixth period	_____

Unit 8c

Materials required

• Map of your campus on an overhead transparency (optional).

• Reprints of the masters provided.

• Unit pictures.

Introduction

• Introduce vocabulary and terms using Guessing and the instructor's set of picture cards, or the map of the buildings of your campus on the overhead projector.

Comprehension Drills

• Use Picture-card drills. As an alternative (or a follow-up), have students call out the names of various buildings on campus as you describe them in Chinese.

Oral Practice

• The students form pairs. Each receives a copy of "What are you doing where?" and completes the tasks assigned.

• Have the students listen to the audiotape and complete the Dialog Practice exercise for homework. Check in class.

• Divide the class into groups of 3 to rehearse "Looking for David." Have one group perform for the class.

• Brainstorm for variations of the sample statements and questions provided on the vocabulary sheet.

Controlled use

• The students form pairs. Each receives a copy of "What is this place?" and completes the tasks assigned.

Unit 8c: What are you doing where?

1. Fill in the blanks below with a selection from the list of activities provided. Do not select any activity more than once.

	(Your answer)	(Your partner's answer)
Wǒ dào jiàoshì qù.....	_____	_____
Wǒ dào dàlǐtáng qù.....	_____	_____
Wǒ dào shíyànshì qù.....	_____	_____
Wǒ dào cāntīng qù.....	_____	_____
Wǒ dào tǐyùguǎn qù.....	_____	_____
Wǒ dào cāochǎng qù.....	_____	_____
Wǒ dào yóuyǒngchí qù.....	_____	_____
Wǒ dào bàngōngshì qù.....	_____	_____
Wǒ dào sùshè qù.....	_____	_____

Activities:

bànshì
chī zǎofàn (wǔfàn, wǎnfàn)
dǎ lánqiú (páiqiú)
niànshū
shàngkè
shuìjiào
tī zúqiú (Měiguó zúqiú)
tīng yánjiǎng
xiūxi
yóuyǒng
zhǎo péngyǒu *look for a friend*
zuò shíyàn
zuò tǐcāo

2. Now find out what your partner has selected by asking questions such as "Nǐ dào jiàoshì qù zuò shénme? Nǐ dào tǐyùguǎn qù dǎ qiú ma? Shénme qiú?" etc. Write the answers in the spaces provided.

Unit 8c: What is this place? (A)

You have 7 minutes to describe the pictures below (entirely in Chinese) to your partner, <u>without mentioning the name of the item</u>. S/he will guess what it is, and if correct, will write the name of the item in the corresponding blanks provided on his/her sheet of paper. Do as many as you can within the time allotment. Then reverse roles for the next 7 minutes; guess what your partner is describing, and write your answers in the blanks on your form.

a. Describe the following:

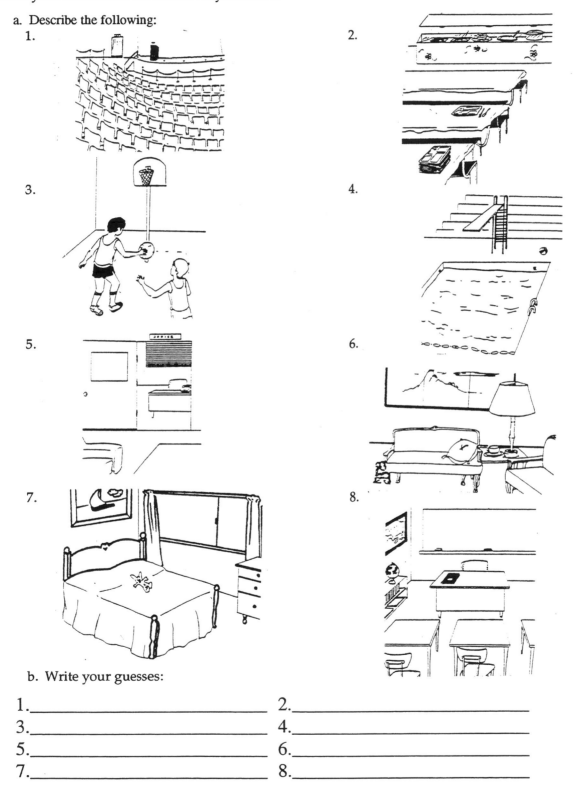

b. Write your guesses:

1._____ 2._____

3._____ 4._____

5._____ 6._____

7._____ 8._____

Unit 8c: What is this place? (B)

Your partner will describe a number of places to you. Guess what they are, and if correct, write their names in the blanks provided below. Do as many as you can within 7 minutes. Then reverse roles for the next 7 mintes. Describe the pictures below (entirely in Chinese) to your partner, <u>without mentioning the name of the place</u>.

a. Write your guesses:

1._____   2._____
3._____   4._____
5._____   6._____
7._____   8._____

b. Describe the following:

1.

2.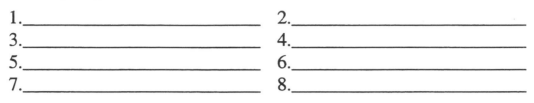

3.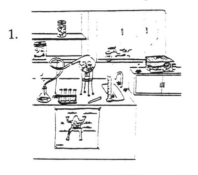

4.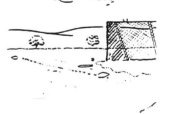

5.

6.

7.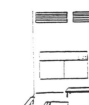

8.

Unit 8d

Materials required

•List of the faculty, staff, and administrators of your school (optional).

•Copies of the class roster, one for each student.

•Reprints of the masters provided.

•Unit pictures.

Introduction

•Use Guessing with the instructor's set of picture-cards, or the list of your faculty and staff.

Comprehension Drills

•Use Picture-card drills. As an alternative (or a follow-up), have students call out the names of various individuals on campus as you describe them in Chinese.

Oral Practice

•The students form pairs. Each receives a copy of "IDs" (cut apart the sheet at the dotted line, and give one half to each student) and takes turns interviewing his or her partner to fill in all the information requested. When the students reassemble as a class, have each student say something about the person he or she has just interviewed (Ta zui hao de pengyou jiao Robin. Ta meiyou tongwu.)

•Have the students listen to the audiotape and complete the Dialog Practice exercise for homework. Check in class.

•Divide the class into groups of 3 to rehearse "Gossip." Have 1-2 groups perform.

•Brainstorm for variations of the sample statements and questions provided.

Controlled use

•The class role-plays members of Xiao Wang's school or college. Hand out one copy of the class roster to each student. Then make as many copies of "Who are you? (Handout #1)" as necessary, so that each student in your class can have one of the 16 slips provided (cut them apart). Remember not to have more than one principal or best friend for Xiao Wang. Also, remember not to reinforce sexual stereotyping by purposely giving the "principal/president" slip to a male student and the "secretary" slip to a female student; it would be best to cover yourself by distributing the slips at random, or by having each student blindly pick a slip from a bunch in your hand.

Make enough copies of "Who are you? (Handout #2)" to provide one slip to each student in your class.

Have them complete the task assigned, making notes on the roster about what each of their classmates is playing.

Check their work by asking students what role each of their classmates is playing.

Unit 8d: IDs

Have your partner respond to each of the questions below by rephrasing it in Chinese. Fill in the blanks as best you can.

Name of the principal/president of your school: _____

Name a dean: _____

Name a department chair: _____

Name a teacher other than your Chinese teacher: _____

Name a librarian: _____

Name a secretary: _____

Name a custodian: _____

Name a classmate of yours: _____

Name your best friend: _____

Name your boy/girl friend: _____

Name your room-mate: _____

Have your partner respond to each of the questions below by rephrasing it in Chinese. Fill in the blanks as best you can.

Name of the principal/president of your school: _____

Name a dean: _____

Name a department chair: _____

Name a teacher other than your Chinese teacher: _____

Name a librarian: _____

Name a secretary: _____

Name a custodian: _____

Name a classmate of yours: _____

Name your best friend: _____

Name your boy/girl friend: _____

Name your room-mate: _____

Unit 8d: Who are you? (handout #1)

- -

You are the principal in Xiǎo Wáng's school.

- -

You are a dean in Xiǎo Wáng's school.

- -

You are a department chair in Xiǎo Wáng's school.

- -

You are a department chair in Xiǎo Wáng's school.

- -

You are a department chair in Xiǎo Wáng's school.

- -

You are a teacher in Xiǎo Wáng's school.

- -

You are a librarian in Xiǎo Wáng's school.

- -

You are a librarian in Xiǎo Wáng's school.

- -

You are a secretary in Xiǎo Wáng's school.

- -

You are a secretary in Xiǎo Wáng's school.

- -

You are a custodian in Xiǎo Wáng's school.

- -

You are a student in Xiǎo Wáng's school.

- -

You are a student in Xiǎo Wáng's school; you are Xiǎo Wáng's best friend.

- -

You are a student in Xiǎo Wáng's school; you are Xiǎo Wáng's classmate

- -

You are a student in Xiǎo Wáng's school; you are Xiǎo Wáng's classmate.

- -

You are a student in Xiǎo Wáng's school; you are Xiǎo Wáng's roommate.

Unit 8d: Who are you? (handout #2)

Each person in the class is a member of Xiao Wáng's school. Some are faculty and staff; others are students. Find out what each of your classmates is. Sample exchanges:

Q: Nǐ shì Xiǎo Wáng xuéxiào de shénme rén? A: Wǒ shì tāmen xuéxiào de jiàowù zhǔrèn.
Q: Nǐ shì Xiǎo Wáng xuéxiào de shénme rén? A: Wǒ shì tāmen xuéxiào de xuéshēng.

If someone identifies themselves as a student, find out whether or not they are Xiao Wang's classmate, best friend, or roommate.

Each person in the class is a member of Xiao Wáng's school. Some are faculty and staff; others are students. Find out what each of your classmates is. Sample exchanges:

Q: Nǐ shì Xiǎo Wáng xuéxiào de shénme rén? A: Wǒ shì tāmen xuéxiào de jiàowù zhǔrèn.
Q: Nǐ shì Xiǎo Wáng xuéxiào de shénme rén? A: Wǒ shì tāmen xuéxiào de xuéshēng.

If someone identifies themselves as a student, find out whether or not they are Xiao Wang's classmate, best friend, or roommate.

Each person in the class is a member of Xiao Wáng's school. Some are faculty and staff; others are students. Find out what each of your classmates is. Sample exchanges:

Q: Nǐ shì Xiǎo Wáng xuéxiào de shénme rén? A: Wǒ shì tāmen xuéxiào de jiàowù zhǔrèn.
Q: Nǐ shì Xiǎo Wáng xuéxiào de shénme rén? A: Wǒ shì tāmen xuéxiào de xuéshēng.

If someone identifies themselves as a student, find out whether or not they are Xiao Wang's classmate, best friend, or roommate.

Each person in the class is a member of Xiao Wáng's school. Some are faculty and staff; others are students. Find out what each of your classmates is. Sample exchanges:

Q: Nǐ shì Xiǎo Wáng xuéxiào de shénme rén? A: Wǒ shì tāmen xuéxiào de jiàowù zhǔrèn.
Q: Nǐ shì Xiǎo Wáng xuéxiào de shénme rén? A: Wǒ shì tāmen xuéxiào de xuéshēng.

If someone identifies themselves as a student, find out whether or not they are Xiao Wang's classmate, best friend, or roommate.

Each person in the class is a member of Xiao Wáng's school. Some are faculty and staff; others are students. Find out what each of your classmates is. Sample exchanges:

Q: Nǐ shì Xiǎo Wáng xuéxiào de shénme rén? A: Wǒ shì tāmen xuéxiào de jiàowù zhǔrèn.
Q: Nǐ shì Xiǎo Wáng xuéxiào de shénme rén? A: Wǒ shì tāmen xuéxiào de xuéshēng.

If someone identifies themselves as a student, find out whether or not they are Xiao Wang's classmate, best friend, or roommate.

Unit 9a

Materials required

•Student's sheet of picture cards reproduced on an overhead transparency.

•Reprints of the masters provided.

•Unit pictures.

Introduction

•Use Pantomime or Guessing with the unit pictures.

Comprehension Drills

•Use Picture-card drills.

Oral Practice

•The students form pairs. Each receives a copy of "My diet," and completes the tasks assigned.

•Have the students listen to the audiotape and complete the Dialog Practice exercise for homework. Check in class.

•Divide the class into pairs to rehearse "Food for dinner." Have one or two pairs perform for the rest of the class.

•Brainstorm for variations of the sample statements and questions provided on the vocabulary sheet.

Controlled use

•Have your students form small groups of three, four, or five students each.

Project the student's sheet of picture cards on the overhead projector, to serve as the "menu" for this activity.

Photocopy as many of "Ordering (handout #1)" as you need, to match the number of and kind of groups you have. Cut the slips apart and distribute them within each group.

Make copies of "Ordering (handout #2)," cut them apart, and distribute one slip to each student. Have them complete the task assigned.

Check each person's selections.

The correct choices are chicken, crab, vegetables, and fried noodles.

Unit 9a: My diet.

You and your partner will discuss what you ate yesterday.

a. What did you eat yesterday? Fill in the blanks with selections from the choices listed bottom of the page.

b. Find out what your partner ate yesterday, and list below, in at the English.

Zuótiān wǒ yìtiān *(one day, in the course of the day)* chīle zhèixiē dōngxi:

Ní zuótiān chīle yìxiē shénme?

Nǐ zǎocān chīle shénme?

Wó zǎocān chīle _____

_____

_____

_____

_____

_____

Ní wǔcān chīle shénme?

Wó wǔcān chīle _____

_____

_____

_____

_____

_____

Ní wǎncān chīle shénme?

Wó wǎncān chīle _____

_____

_____

_____

_____

_____

niúròu	yú	shùcài	mǐfàn (báifàn)
zhūròu	xiā	shuíguǒ	chǎofàn
jī	lóngxiā	dòufu	miàntiáo
yā	pángxiè	jīdàn	miànbāo

Unit 9a: Ordering (handout #1)

Use this set for a group of five students:

- -

You hate beef, you are allergic to shrimp, and you are sick of salad.

- -

You hate pork, you are allergic to lobster, and you are sick of soup noodles.

- -

You hate duck, you have sworn never to eat fish, and you hate fruit.

- -

You hate fried rice, you think tofu is disgusting, and you are sick of bread.

- -

You hate plain rice, you are allergic to eggs, and you hate fruit.

- -

Use this set for a group of four students:

- -

You hate beef, you are allergic to shrimp, and you can't stand fried rice.

- -

You hate pork, you are allergic to lobster, you are sick of bread, and you won't eat salad.

- -

You hate duck, you have sworn never to eat fish, and you are allergic to eggs.

- -

You hate the taste of tofu, you can't stand fruit, and you don't like plain rice or soup noodles.

- -

Use this set for a group of three students:

- -

You hate beef, you are allergic to shrimp, and you can't stand salad or any kind of rice.

- -

You hate pork, you are allergic to lobster, and you are sick of bread, tofu, and soup noodles.

- -

You hate duck, you have sworn never to eat fish, you are allergic to eggs, and you hate fruit.

- -

Unit 9a: Ordering (handout #2)

Your group is ordering a meal. Select one dish that is meat or poultry, one that is a fish or seafood, one that is vegetarian, and one that is a starch. Make sure you take into account the food preferences of everyone in your group.

Write your selections here: _____   _____

_____   _____

Your group is ordering a meal. Select one dish that is meat or poultry, one that is a fish or seafood, one that is vegetarian, and one that is a starch. Make sure you take into account the food preferences of everyone in your group.

Write your selections here: _____   _____

_____   _____

Your group is ordering a meal. Select one dish that is meat or poultry, one that is a fish or seafood, one that is vegetarian, and one that is a starch. Make sure you take into account the food preferences of everyone in your group.

Write your selections here: _____   _____

_____   _____

Your group is ordering a meal. Select one dish that is meat or poultry, one that is a fish or seafood, one that is vegetarian, and one that is a starch. Make sure you take into account the food preferences of everyone in your group.

Write your selections here: _____   _____

_____   _____

Your group is ordering a meal. Select one dish that is meat or poultry, one that is a fish or seafood, one that is vegetarian, and one that is a starch. Make sure you take into account the food preferences of everyone in your group.

Write your selections here: _____   _____

_____   _____

Your group is ordering a meal. Select one dish that is meat or poultry, one that is a fish or seafood, one that is vegetarian, and one that is a starch. Make sure you take into account the food preferences of everyone in your group.

Write your selections here: _____   _____

_____   _____

Unit 9b

Materials required

- Reprints of the masters provided.
- Unit pictures.

Introduction

- Use Pantomime as far as it will go. For <u>lu</u> and <u>hongshao,</u> the instructor set of picture cards with a verbal explanation may be necessary. Creative props (such as slides of the cooking process and the product; a video segment of a culinary show; or a taste of the product from your own kitchen) would be enriching (but not essential).

Comprehension Drills

- Use Picture-card drills.

Oral Practice

- The students form pairs. One of the pair receives "How do you cook it? (A)" and the other receives "How do you cook it? (B)"; together, they complete the task assigned.

- Have the students listen to the audiotape and complete the Dialog Practice exercise for homework. Check in class.

- Divide the class into groups of four to rehearse "Eating out." Have one or two groups perform for the rest of the class.

- Brainstorm for variations of the sample statements and questions provided on the vocabulary sheet.

Controlled use

- Make as many copies of "Pricing the foodstalls (handout #1)" as there are students in your class. Distribute one copy per student.

Make one copy of "Pricing the foodstalls (handout #2)" for every 30 students in your class. Cut apart and distribute the slips evenly among the students. Each slips tells what the student is selling at what price.

Using Inner/outer circles or Mingling, have the students complete the task assigned.

Unit 9b: How do you cook it? (A)

The titles arranged horizontally indicate types of foods: eggs, chicken, pork, beef, and vegetables. The titles listed vertically indicate styles of preparation: pan-fried, stir-fried, deep-fried, boiled, steamed, stewed, baked (roasted, grilled), and red-cooked. Each cell in the grid indicates a certain food prepared a certain way. The name of a dish appearing in a cell indicates that this style of preparation for this food is common in China.

You have information on your grid that your partner does not, and vice versa. Work with your partner to complete the grid. Cells that neither of you have information for should be left blank: the dish does not commonly exist.

Ask questions such as "Yǒu jiānde jīdàn ma? Yóu chǎode jī ma?" Answers would be: "Yǒu, jiàozuò *Jiāndàn* "; "Yǒu, jiàozuò *Chǎo jīdīng*."

	jīdàn	jī	ròu	niúròu	shùcài
jiān	jiān dàn				
chǎo	chǎo dàn	chǎo jīdīng		chǎo niúròu sī	
zhá			zhá ròu		
zhǔ			zhǔ ròu	zhǔ niúròu	
zhēng	zhēng dàn		zhēng ròupiàn		zhēng shùcài
lǔ		lǔ jīkuài	lǔ ròu		
kǎo				kǎo niúròu	
hóngshāo			hóngshāo ròu		

Unit 9b: How do you cook it? (B)

The titles arranged horizontally indicate types of foods: eggs, chicken, pork, beef, and vegetables. The titles listed vertically indicate styles of preparation: pan-fried, stir-fried, deep-fried, boiled, steamed, stewed, baked (roasted, grilled), and red-cooked. Each cell in the grid indicates a certain food prepared a certain way. The name of a dish appearing in a cell indicates that this style of preparation for this food is common in China.

You have information on your grid that your partner does not, and vice versa. Work with your partner to complete the grid. Cells that neither of you have information for should be left blank: the dish does not commonly exist.

Ask questions such as "Yǒu jiānde jīdàn ma? Yóu chǎode jī ma?" Answers would be: "Yǒu, jiàozuò *Jiāndàn* "; "Yǒu, jiàozuò *Chǎo jīdīng*."

	jīdàn	jī	ròu	niúròu	shùcài
jiān	jiān jīpiàn				
chǎo			chǎo ròusī		chǎo shùcài
zhá		zhá jīkuài		zhá niúpái	
zhǔ	zhǔ dàn	zhǔ jī			zhǔ shùcài
zhēng		zhēng jīkuài		zhēng niúròu	
lǔ	lǔ dàn			lǔ niúròu	
kǎo		kǎo ji	kǎo ròu		
hóngshāo				hóngshāo niúròu	

Unit 9b: Pricing the foodstalls (handout #1)

You are living in a Chinese community. You are making a list of some available foods and their prices at foodstalls in a local marketplace, to help out a friend who will be moving here soon. Each student in the class will roleplay a vendor of a particular food. Go around the room, and find out what each of the following items costs.

fried eggs	scrambled eggs	deep fried chicken
_____	_____	_____
steamed chicken	baked chicken	stewed chicken
_____	_____	_____
stir-fried chicken cubes	red-cooked fish	steamed fish
_____	_____	_____
deep fried fish	pan-fried fish	stir-fried slices of fish
_____	_____	_____
baked fish	stewed beef	roasted (baked) beef
_____	_____	_____
stir-fried beef slivers	red-cooked beef	red-cooked pork
_____	_____	_____
stir-fried pork slivers	steamed pork	boiled crab
_____	_____	_____
boiled lobster	steamed crab	steamed lobster
_____	_____	_____
stir-fried shrimp	deep-fried shrimp	steamed shrimp
_____	_____	_____
stir-fried vegetables	steamed vegetables	steamed tofu
_____	_____	_____

Unit 9b: Pricing the foodstalls (handout #2)

jiān jīdàn .80¥	chǎo jīdàn .85¥	zhá jīkuài 3.00¥
zhēng jīkuài 2.75¥	kǎo jī 5.00¥	lǔ jīkuài 3.50¥
chǎo jīdīng 3.50¥	hóngshāo yú 9.00¥	zhēng yú 8.50¥
zhá yúkuài 5.50¥	jiān yú 6.75¥	chǎo yúpiàn 5.95¥
kǎo yú 9.75¥	kǎo niúròu 7.75¥	lǔ niúròu 4.90¥
chǎo niúròusī 4.95¥	hóngshāo niúròu 8.50¥	hóngshāo ròu 7.00¥
chǎo ròusī 5.25¥	zhēng ròu 5.15¥	zhǔ pángxiè 9.50¥
zhǔ lóngxiā 15.00¥	zhēng pángxiè 10.00¥	zhēng lóngxiā 17.00¥
chǎo xiā 6.95¥	zhá xiā 5.50¥	zhēng xiā 6.80¥
chǎo shùcài 3.50¥	zhēng shùcài 3.75¥	zhēng dòufu 4.00¥

Unit 9c

Materials required

•Reprints of the masters provided.

•Unit pictures.

Introduction

•This unit is best introduced at a well-stocked Chinese buffet, but in lieu of that, Guessing using the instructor's set of picture-cards will suffice.

Comprehension Drills

•Use Picture-card drills.

Oral Practice

•*Photocopy "Facts about Food" onto an overhead transparency.*

The class divides into two teams. Put "Facts about Food" on the overhead projector, revealing and reading aloud only the first prompt: ...shì xián de. The first student who raises a hand with an answer to fill in the blank (Qingzheng yú shì xián de; Zhá jikuài shì xián de; etc.) obtains a turn for his or her team. Thereafter the turns alternate from team to team. Each has no more than 5 seconds (or 3 seconds) to respond (keep time by clapping your hands or pounding the table: clap clap clap clap CLAP—on the final clap the turn is over). When responses to the prompt have been exhausted, the LAST TEAM to PROVIDE A CORRECT RESPONSE wins a point. Proceed to the next cue. Add your own cues as necessary, until one team wins the game.

•Have the students listen to the audiotape and complete the Dialog Practice exercise for homework. Check in class.

•Divide the class into groups of four to rehearse "Eating out (continued)." Have one or two groups perform for the rest of the class.

•Brainstorm for variations of the sample statements and questions provided on the vocabulary sheet.

Controlled use

•The students form small groups of 2-3. Each group secretly things of one "favorite dish," the other groups take turns asking questions in "Twenty Questions" format to guess what the dish is. Questions might include: Shì ji ma? Shì niúròu ma? Shì kaode ma? Tiánbùtián? Suanbùsuan? Litóu you shucài ma? Continue until all dishes have been guessed; go another round if time permits.

Unit 9c: Facts about food

...shì xián de.

...yǒu yìdiǎr tián.

...yǒu yìdiǎr suān.

...yǒu yìdiǎr là.

...shì yú zuò de.

...shì ròu zuò de.

...shì niúròu zuò de.

...shì jī zuò de.

...shì zhēng de.

...shì chǎo de.

...shì zhǔ de.

...shì kǎo de.

Unit 9d

Materials required

•Optional: assemble a set of the following—a teabag or an empty container of Chinese tea leaves; a styrofoam or paper coffee cup; an empty can of orange juice; an empty can of Coke; an empty container of fruit punch; an empty carton of milk; an empty can of beer; an empty bottle of wine (a single serving size such as those served on airlines would be nice); an empty bottle of Maotai liquor (or a picture of one); a plastic bowl, cup, plate, fork, knife, and spoon; disposable chopsticks; a paper napkin; a take-out menu from a Chinese restaurant; a bill from a Chinese restaurant.

•Several packs of "Post-it" stick-on note-pads (the smallest size available, no more than 2" x 2").

•A manila folder for each student in the class.

•Reprints of the masters provided.

•Unit pictures.

Introduction

•Use Guessing with the realia you have assembled, or with the unit pictures.

Comprehension Drills

•Use Picture-card drills. As an alternative or follow-up, substitute the realia for the picture-cards; students either point at objects placed around the classroom, or gather around the objects placed on the teacher's table, and pick up specific ones as directed.

Oral Practice

•Pass out approximately 20 "Post-it" stick-on notes to each student. Dictate the vocabulary listed on "Give it to me" to the class, and have them write each item separately (and clearly and neatly) on a "Post-it" note. In all, they should end up with 19 completed notes.

Distribute one copy of "Give it to me" and one manila folder to each student.

Divide the class into two teams.

Members of one team roleplay waiters and waitresses. They take the "Post-it" notes they have made and neatly cover each item on "Give it to me" with the corresponding "Post-it" note. When the sheet is covered with "Post-it" notes, they insert it into their manila folders, and prepare to go from patron to patron, seeing to their needs.

Members of the other team roleplay patrons. They put away their "Post-it" notes until the next round, insert "Give it to me" into their manila folders, seat themselves in a circle, and wait for a waiter or waitress to come to them.

The waiters/waitresses go Inner circle/outer circle style (see Introduction) from patron to patron. Each patron may request one item: <u>Qing gei wo yìdiar chá; Qing gei wo yíge beizi; Qing ba zhàngdan gei wo</u>. The waiter/waitress complies by pulling off the appropriate "Post-it" note and handing it to the patron, repeating the name of the item in doing so: <u>Zhè shì chá; Zhè shì beizi; Zhè shì zhàngdan</u>. Then s/he moves on to the next patron. If the item the patron requests has already been given away, the waiter/waitress responds: <u>Dùibuqi, méiyou le</u>, and the patron must request something else.

Each item the patron receives is then pressed onto the sheet "Give it to me." The patron's goal is to cover every printed item with an appropriate "Post-it" note.

The goal of the waiters/waitresses is to give away every "Post-it" note to a patron who needs it. Check to see that patrons and waitpersons have achieved their objectives.

In the next round, teams exchange roles.

• Have the students listen to the audiotape and complete the Dialog Practice exercise for homework. Check in class.

• Divide the class into groups of four to rehearse "Eating out Western style." Have one or two groups perform for the rest of the class.

• Brainstorm for variations of the sample statements and questions provided.

Controlled use

• The students form pairs. One of the pair receives "Hosting a party (patron)," and the other receives "Hosting a party (waiter/waitress)." They complete the task assigned.

Unit 9d: Give it to me

Waiters/ waitresses: Cover each of the items below with your corresponding "Post-it" note, and then insert this sheet into your manila folder. Go from patron to patron, asking "Nín yào shénme ma?" Give the patron what s/he asks for by pulling your "Post-it" note off and handing it over. If the note has already been given away, say "Dùibuqi, méiyou le." Your goal is to give away all your "Post-it" notes, but you can only hand over one when a patron requests it.

Patrons: Insert this sheet into your manila folder. There should be no "Post-it" notes affixed to it when you begin this activity. As each waiter/waitress comes to you, make a request for one of the items below: Qǐng gěi wǒ yīdiar chá; Qǐng gěi wǒ yīge bēizi; Qǐng bǎ zhàngdān gěi wǒ. When you receive the note denoting that item, use it to cover the printed item below. If what you want is not available with one particular waiter/ waitress, ask for something else. Your goal is to cover every item with a "Post-it" note.

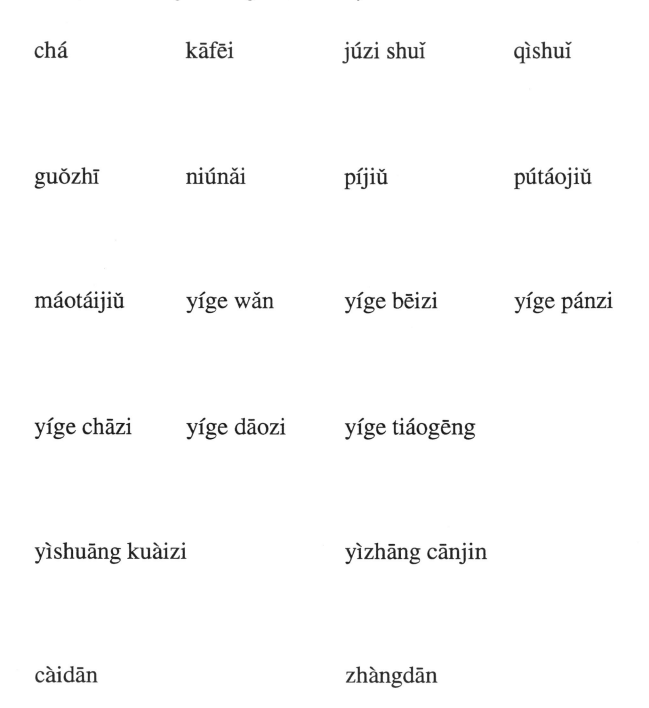

| chá | kāfēi | júzi shuǐ | qìshuǐ |

| guǒzhī | niúnǎi | píjiǔ | pútáojiǔ |

| máotáijiǔ | yíge wǎn | yíge bēizi | yíge pánzi |

| yíge chāzi | yíge dāozi | yíge tiáogēng |

| yìshuāng kuàizi | | yìzhāng cānjin |

| càidān | | zhàngdān |

Unit 9d: Hosting a party (patron)

You are taking seven friends to lunch at a Chinese restaurant in America. You want to order eight dishes (for the eight of you), plus rice or noodles, and drinks for all. You want to spend approximately $100 (but no more) on the food (plus $20 for tax and tip). The menu that you have been given has no prices on it. Consult with your waiter/waitress, and then decide what you are going to order. Write your order on the tally sheet below, and tally up your total charge.

Check here to order:

Beef (Cost:_____) _____ Charge: $_____

Pork (Cost:_____) _____ Charge: $_____

Chicken (Cost:_____) _____ Charge: $_____

Fish (Cost:_____) _____ Charge: $_____

Duck (Cost:_____) _____ Charge: $_____

Lobster (Cost:_____) _____ Charge: $_____

Crab (Cost:_____) _____ Charge: $_____

Shrimp (Cost:_____) _____ Charge: $_____

Tofu (Cost:_____) _____ Charge: $_____

Vegetables (Cost:_____) _____ Charge: $_____

Noodles (Cost:_____) _____ Charge: $_____

How many do you want?

Rice (plain) (Cost:_____) _____ Charge: $_____

Fruit (Cost:_____) _____ Charge: $_____

Beer (Cost:_____) _____ Charge: $_____

Wine (Cost:_____) _____ Charge: $_____

Orange juice (Cost:_____) _____ Charge: $_____

Soda (Cost:_____) _____ Charge: $_____

Milk (Cost:_____) _____ Charge: $_____

Tea (Cost:_____) _____ Charge: $_____

Total Charge: $_____

Unit 9d: Hosting a party (waiter/waitress)

You are taking an order for someone who is treating seven friends to lunch at a Chinese restaurant in America. He/she wants to order eight dishes plus rice or noodles, and drinks. The menu you have given the customer has no prices on it. Consult with him/her, and then write down the order on the tally sheet below. Add up the total charge.

Check here to order:

Beef ($8.95)   _____   Charge: $_____

Pork ($6.50)   _____   Charge: $_____

Chicken ($6.25)   _____   Charge: $_____

Fish ($9.95)   _____   Charge: $_____

Duck ($7.75)   _____   Charge: $_____

Lobster ($23.95)   _____   Charge: $_____

Crab ($15.00)   _____   Charge: $_____

Shrimp ($8.75)   _____   Charge: $_____

Tofu ($3.50)   _____   Charge: $_____

Vegetables ($4.75)   _____   Charge: $_____

Noodles ($4.95)   _____   Charge: $_____

How many do you want?

Rice (plain) ($.70/serving)   _____   Charge: $_____

Beer ($1.00/bottle)   _____   Charge: $_____

Wine ($1.25/glass)   _____   Charge: $_____

Orange juice ($1.10/glass)   _____   Charge: $_____

Soda ($.60/glass)   _____   Charge: $_____

Milk ($.85/glass)   _____   Charge: $_____

Fruit ($1.00/serving)   _____   Charge: $_____

Tea (free)   _____   Charge: $_____

Total Charge: $_____

Unit 10a

Materials required

• Blank 5" x 8" index cards, magic marker.

• Reprints of the masters provided.

• Unit pictures.

Introduction

• Use Pantomime, or Guessing with the instructor's set of picture-cards.

Comprehension Drills

• Use Picture-card drills.

Oral Practice

• *Write each of the place-names in this unit on one index card.*

This activity, as it stands, is for a class of 17 students. See below for suggestions for handling a class with fewer or more than 17 students.

Arrange 16 seats in a circle, facing inwards. Tape a place-card to each seat, so that the card is clearly visible even when someone is sitting in the seat. (If the seats have table surfaces attached, hang the card from the front of that. If the chair is simply a chair, turn it around so that it faces the rear of the room, and attach the card to the rear of the backrest.) Stand in the middle of the circle; have 16 of your students take seats facing you. One student will be left standing with you.

Instruct this student to go and displace any one of the others (say the student in the seat labelled feijichang, which is the 3rd seat from some predetermined point in the circle) by saying "Ni qu ba" or "Ni qu zuo ba". Student #1 sits down, displacing student #2, who walks to the center of the circle. There student #2 has the following conversation with the teacher.

Teacher:	Ni cong nar lai?
Student #2:	Wo cong feijichang lai.
Teacher:	Feijichang li zher yuan ma?
Student #2:	Bu hen yuan.
Teacher:	Jili lu?
Student #2:	Sanli lu. *(This response reflects the relative order of the seat: the 3rd seat = 3 miles away.)*
Teacher:	Ni xianzai dao nar qu?
Student #2:	*(selects one of the seats at random)* Wo dao tushuguan qu.
Teacher:	Zaijian.
Student #2:	Laoshi, zaijian.

Thereupon student #2 walks to the seat marked tushuguan and displaces student #3, who walks to the front of the class, and has the same conversation with the teacher. At some point, you may wish to ask for a volunteer to take your place in the conversation.

Teacher:	Ni cong nar lai?
Student #3:	Wo cong tushuguan lai.

Continue until several people have had a shot at the conversation. This is a rather mechanical, form-oriented activity, so it would be best not to continue it more than 5-10 minutes.

If you have more than 17 in the class, make duplicate place cards and increase the number of chairs. If you have less than 17, leave some of the place cards out; swap these with some that are in use, at some point in the activity.

•Have the students listen to the audiotape and complete the Dialog Practice exercise for homework. Check in class.

•Divide the class into groups of 4 to rehearse "Visitors." Have 1-2 groups perform.

•Brainstorm for variations of the sample statements and questions provided.

Controlled use

•The students form pairs. One of each pair receives "That's where I'm going (A)," and the other receives "That's where I'm going (B)." They complete the task assigned.

Unit 10a: That's where I'm going (A)

In a rigidly planned community of the future, the institutions around town are laid out in concentric circles around City Hall (the black square in the center) in one of four quadrants: North, South, East, and West. Each successive circle is an increment of one mile from the last. Each institution is numbered, from 1 to 16. You were given a key to the numbering system, but in an argument you had with your partner recently, the key was torn, so that you are left with only the even-numbered institutions. Your partner has the odd-numbers. Since you need to visit every institution as part of your job as tax auditor/city planner, you are on the telephone to your partner (both of you have offices in City Hall, which is a very large building), to obtain the rest of the information you need.

Fill in each of the squares on the concentric circles with a number representing a place, based on the information you possess and on what your partner tells you.

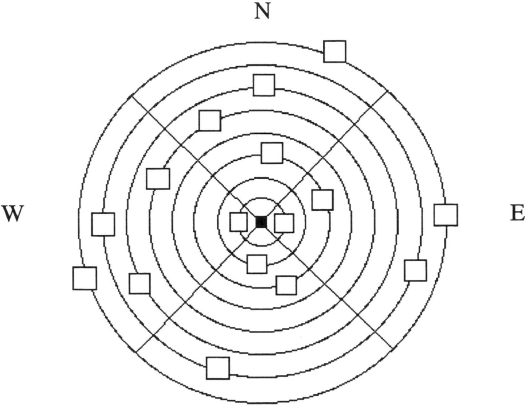

You want to go to the following places:

              Quadrant?   Distance from City Hall?

1. The train station _____ _____

3. The restaurant _____ _____

5. The theater _____ _____

7. The school _____ _____

9. The bookstore _____ _____

11. The bank _____ _____

13. The gas station _____ _____

15. The hospital _____ _____

You know about the following places:

#2, the airport, is in the North, 3 miles from City Hall.

#4, the post office, is in the East, 1 mile from City Hall.

#6, the cinema, is in the South, 4 miles from City Hall.

#8, the hotel, is in the East, 8 miles from City Hall.

#10, the library, is in the West, 8 miles from City Hall.

#12, the bus stop, is in the West, 5 miles from City Hall.

#14, the market, is in the South, 7 miles from City Hall.

#16, the police station, is in the West, 1 mile from City Hall.

Unit 10a: That's where I'm going (B)

In a rigidly planned community of the future, the institutions around town are laid out in concentric circles around City Hall (the black square in the center) in one of four quadrants: North, South, East, and West. Each successive circle is an increment of one mile from the last. Each institution is numbered, from 1 to 16. You were given a key to the numbering system, but in an argument you had with your partner recently, the key was torn, so that you are left with only the even-numbered institutions. Your partner has the odd-numbers. Since you need to visit every institution as part of your job as tax auditor/city planner, you are on the telephone to your partner (both of you have offices in City Hall, which is a very large building), to obtain the rest of the information you need.

Fill in each of the squares on the concentric circles with a number representing a place, based on the information you possess and on what your partner tells you.

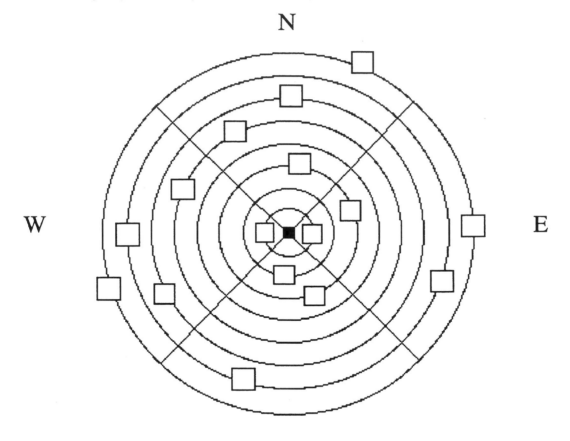

You want to go to the following places:

	Quadrant?	Distance from City Hall?
2.. The airport		
4. The post office		
6. The cinema		
8. The hotel		
10. The library		
12. The bus stop		
14. The market		
16. The police station		

You know about the following places:

#1, the train station, is in the South, 2 miles from City Hall.

#3, the restaurant, is in the West, 6 miles from City Hall.

#5, the theatre, is in the North, 5 miles from City Hall.

#7, the school, is in the East, 3 miles from City Hall.

#9, the bookstore, is in the North, 8 miles from City Hall.

#11, the bank, is in the East, 7 miles from City Hall.

#13, the gas station, is in the West, 7 miles from City Hall.

#15, the hospital, is in the North, 6 miles from City Hall.

Unit 10a: That's where I'm going (key)

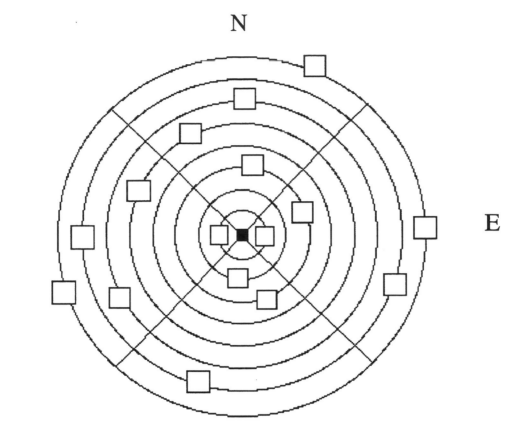

#1, the train station, is in the South, 2 miles from City Hall.

#2, the airport, is in the North, 3 miles from City Hall.

#3, the restaurant, is in the West, 6 miles from City Hall.

#4, the post office, is in the East, 1 mile from City Hall.

#5, the theatre, is in the North, 5 miles from City Hall.

#6, the cinema, is in the South, 4 miles from City Hall.

#7, the school, is in the East, 3 miles from City Hall.

#8, the hotel, is in the East, 8 miles from City Hall.

#9, the bookstore, is in the North, 8 miles from City Hall.

#10, the library, is in the West, 8 miles from City Hall.

#11, the bank, is in the East, 7 miles from City Hall.

#12, the bus stop, is in the West, 5 miles from City Hall.

#13, the gas station, is in the West, 7 miles from City Hall.

#14, the market, is in the South, 7 miles from City Hall.

#15, the hospital, is in the North, 6 miles from City Hall.

#16, the police station, is in the West, 1 mile from City Hall.

Unit 10b

Materials required

• Reprints of the masters provided.

• Unit pictures.

Introduction

• Use Guessing with the instructor's set of picture-cards.

Comprehension Drills

• Use Picture-cards drills.

Oral Practice

• The students form pairs. Each receives a copy of "Where did she go?" and completes the task assigned.

• Have the students listen to the audiotape and complete the Dialog Practice exercise for homework. Check in class.

• Divide the class into groups of 3 to rehearse "David's Parents." Have 1-2 groups perform.

• Brainstorm for variations of the sample statements and questions provided on the vocabulary sheet.

Controlled use

• The students form pairs. Each receives a copy of "When was the last time you went?" and completes the tasks assigned.

Unit 10b: Where did she go?

Match the people on the left at random with the destinations in the middle, and the activities on the right. Record the numbers representing your selections in the column marked A. Then communicate your choices to your partner by linking them together in complete statements.

Example: (1-2-4) Wáng Xiānsheng dào héshàng huáchuán qù le.

(2-6-2) Chén Tàitai dào gōngyuán lǐ sànbù qù le.

Record your partner's choices in the column marked B. Finally, check your accuracy by comparing your figures with your partner's.

A   B

1. Wáng Xiānsheng

2. Chén Tàitai

3. Lǐ Xiáojie

4. Zhāng Nǚshì

5. Lǎo Huáng

6. Xiǎo Zhào

7. Máo Tóngzhì

8. Yán Yīsheng

9. Lín Lǎoshī

10. Wèi Lùshī

1. _____ _____
2. _____ _____
3. _____ _____
4. _____ _____
5. _____ _____
6. _____ _____
7. _____ _____
8. _____ _____
9. _____ _____
10. _____ _____

Unit 10b: When was the last time you went?

Fill in times or dates as you wish, to indicate the LAST TIME you went to each of the locations or to do each of the activities below. Record your answers under Column A. Then converse with your partner to find out what s/he has put down, and record his/her answers under Column B.

Examples: Q: Nǐ zuìjìn *(most recently)* shénme shíhòu dào shānshàng qù guò?
A: Wǒ zuótian dào shānshàng qù guò.
Q: Nǐ zuìjìn shénme shíhòu huá guò chuán?
A: Wǒ shàngge xīngqī huá guò chuán.

	A	B		A	B
Theatre:	_____	_____	Forest:	_____	_____
Downtown:	_____	_____	Park:	_____	_____
Hospital:	_____	_____	Beach:	_____	_____
Gas station:	_____	_____	Lakeshore:	_____	_____
Market:	_____	_____	Mountains:	_____	_____
Library:	_____	_____	Garden:	_____	_____
Post office:	_____	_____	Riverside:	_____	_____
Bank:	_____	_____	Row a boat:	_____	_____
School:	_____	_____	Take a walk:	_____	_____
Busstop:	_____	_____	Go hiking:	_____	_____
Movies:	_____	_____	Window shop:	_____	_____
Police station:	_____	_____	Bookstore:	_____	_____

Unit 10c

Materials required

• Large map of the city, or of a portion of the city, preferably including the vicinity of your school. May be reproduced on an overhead transparency.

• Reprints of the masters provided.

• Unit pictures.

Introduction

• Affix the map to the wall, or project it on the overhead projector. Slowly, recite a narrative of a journey around town, pointing out your route as you speak, with lots of repetition and redundancy to illustrate the meaning of terms you are using.

• Reinforce the meaning of the terms by using Guesswork and the unit pictures.

Comprehension Drills

• Use Picture-card drills. As a follow-up, have volunteers trace your route as you describe a journey around the map.

• Brainstorm for variations of the sample statements and questions provided on the vocabulary sheet.

Oral Practice

• The students form pairs. One member of each pair receives "Taking directions (A)" and the other receives "Taking directions (B)". They complete the tasks assigned.

• Have the students listen to the audiotape and complete the Dialog Practice exercise for homework. Check in class.

• Divide the class into pairs to rehearse "Finding the Post Office." Have one pair perform.

Controlled use

• The students form pairs. One member of each pair receives "Moving out (A)" and the other receives "Moving out (B)". They complete the tasks assigned.

Unit 10c: Taking directions (A)

Below are a set of symbols indicating directions in moving around town. #1 means "go straight," #2 means "go to X street," #3 means "turn left," etc. The Chinese equivalents of most of these directions are given directly below the symbols.

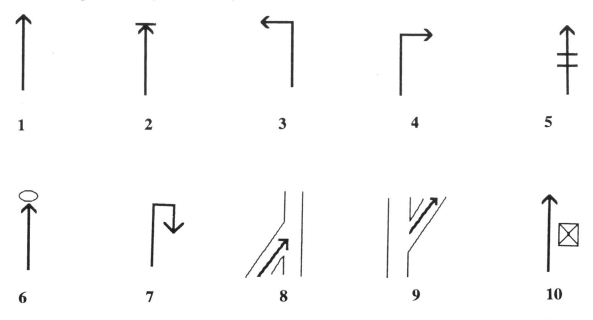

yìzhí zŏu / zŏu dào X jiē / zuó zhuăn / yòu zhuăn / guò liăngge jiēkŏu

zŏu dào dìyíge hónglù dēng / wàng húi zŏu / shàng gāosù gōnglù

xià gāosù gōnglù / jīngguò xuéxiào

Each set of numbers under the column "*A* " below indicates a set of directions. 3-6-4 means "Turn left, go to the first stoplight, then turn right."

Translate the sets of numbers under "*A* " into directions for your partner; s/he will re-encode them into numbers to write down under "*B* ," on his/her sheet.

Then your partner will state directions for your, which you will record the same way, under column "*B* ".

Check your work when you are done by comparing "codes" with your partner .

		A					B		
8	10	9	6	4	___	___	___	___	___
1	5	3	4	3	___	___	___	___	___
8	2	9	7	2	___	___	___	___	___
6	7	10	4	6	___	___	___	___	___
3	4	5	1	2	___	___	___	___	___

Unit 10c: Taking directions (B)

Below are a set of symbols indicating directions in moving around town. #1 means "go straight," #2 means "go to X street," #3 means "turn left," etc. The Chinese equivalents of most of these directions are given directly below the symbols.

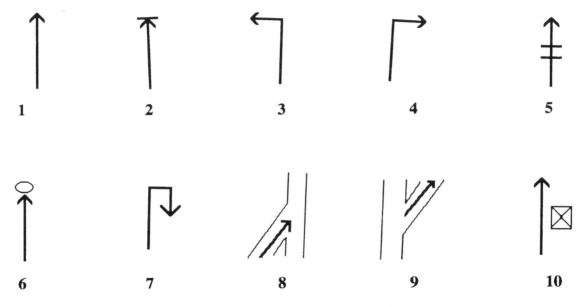

yìzhí zǒu / zǒu dào X jiē / zuó zhuǎn / yòu zhuǎn / guò liǎngge jiēkǒu

zǒu dào dìyíge hónglù dēng / wàng húi zǒu / shàng gāosù gōnglù

xià gāosù gōnglù / jīngguò xuéxiào

Each set of numbers under the column "A" below indicates a set of directions. 3-6-4 means "Turn left, go to the first stoplight, then turn right."

Translate the sets of numbers under "A" into directions for your partner; s/he will re-encode them into numbers to write down under "B," on his/her sheet.

Then your partner will state directions for your, which you will record the same way, under column "B".

Check your work when you are done by comparing "codes" with your partner.

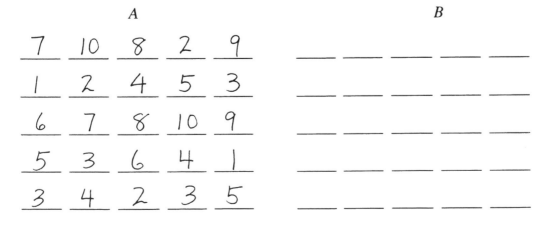

A					B				
7	10	8	2	9					
1	2	4	5	3					
6	7	8	10	9					
5	3	6	4	1					
3	4	2	3	5					

Unit 10c: Moving out (A)

Draw in the location of each of the places on the numbered list below, using the symbols on the bottom of the page. To find out where each place is located, get directions from your partner, starting at the arrow in the bottom right corner of the map. Your partner will also ask you for directions to locations indicated on your map. Begin your directions at the same arrow.

1. train station
2. restaurant
3. bank
4. market
5. gas station
6. hospital

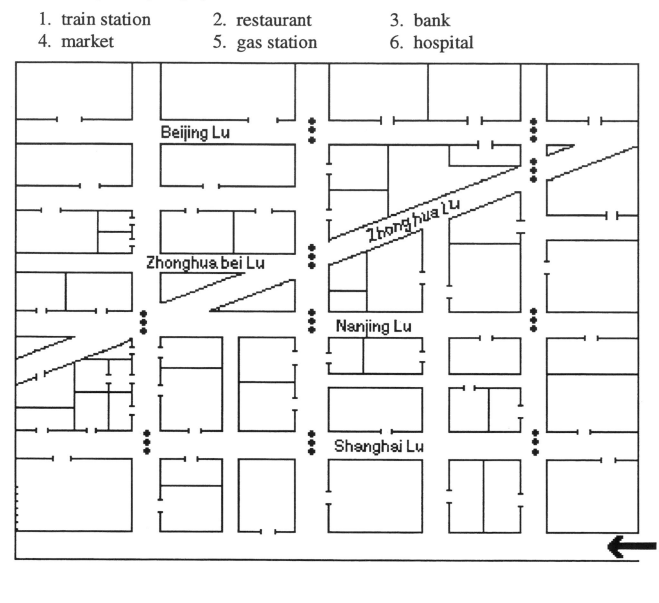

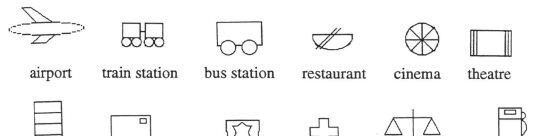

airport   train station   bus station   restaurant   cinema   theatre   bank

hotel   post office   police station   hospital   market   gas station

Unit 10c: Moving out (B)

Draw in the location of each of the places on the numbered list below, using the symbols on the bottom of the page. To find out where each place is located, get directions from your partner, starting at the arrow in the bottom right corner of the map. Your partner will also ask you for directions to locations indicated on your map. Begin your directions at the same arrow.

1. airport
2. bus station
3. cinema
4. hotel
5. post office
6. police station

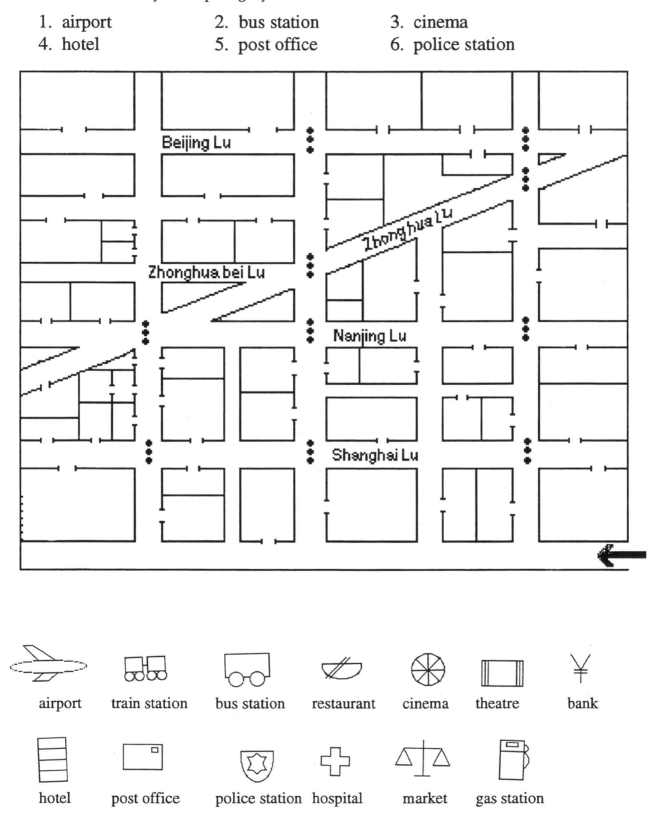

Unit 10d

Materials required
•Reprints of the masters provided.

Introduction
•*Photocopy "China, etc." onto an overhead transparency.*

Project "China, etc." on an overhead projector. Say the names of the places in this lesson, and have volunteers taking turns coming up to the screen and attempting to locate them. Guess-work is welcome; keep repeating the name of a place until someone locates it. If several students try and are unsuccessful at understanding and locating, say, Dongjing, you may wish to help them out by pointing it out to them.

Comprehension Drills
•Have volunteers take turns locating places on "China, etc." as you name and describe them.

Oral Practice
•The students form pairs. Each pair receives one copy of "China, etc." and sets it between them. Student A begins by pointing to a country or city indicated on the map, saying, "Wo yao dao ner qu." Suppose Student A had pointed to the dot representing Beijing. Student B would then clarify, "Ni yao dao Beijing qu ma?" If Student A perceives that Student B has identified the place correctly, s/he would respond, "Dui, wo yao dao Beijing qu."

A disagreement might proceed as follows:

> Student A: Bu, na bushi Beijing.
>
> Student B: Na **shi** Beijing.
>
> Student A: Laoshi, zhe shibushi Beijing?
>
> Teacher: Bu, na shi Shanghai.

Continue the activity for a set period of time, say, 7-10 minutes. The students should say something about every point indicated on the map.

•Have the students listen to the audiotape and complete the Dialog Practice exercise for homework. Check in class.

•Divide the class into groups of 6 to rehearse "Travel Aspirations." Have one group perform for the class.

•Brainstorm for variations of the sample statements and questions provided.

Controlled use
•The students form pairs. One partner receives "Hot and Cold (A)" and the other receives "Hot & Cold (B)." They complete the task assigned.

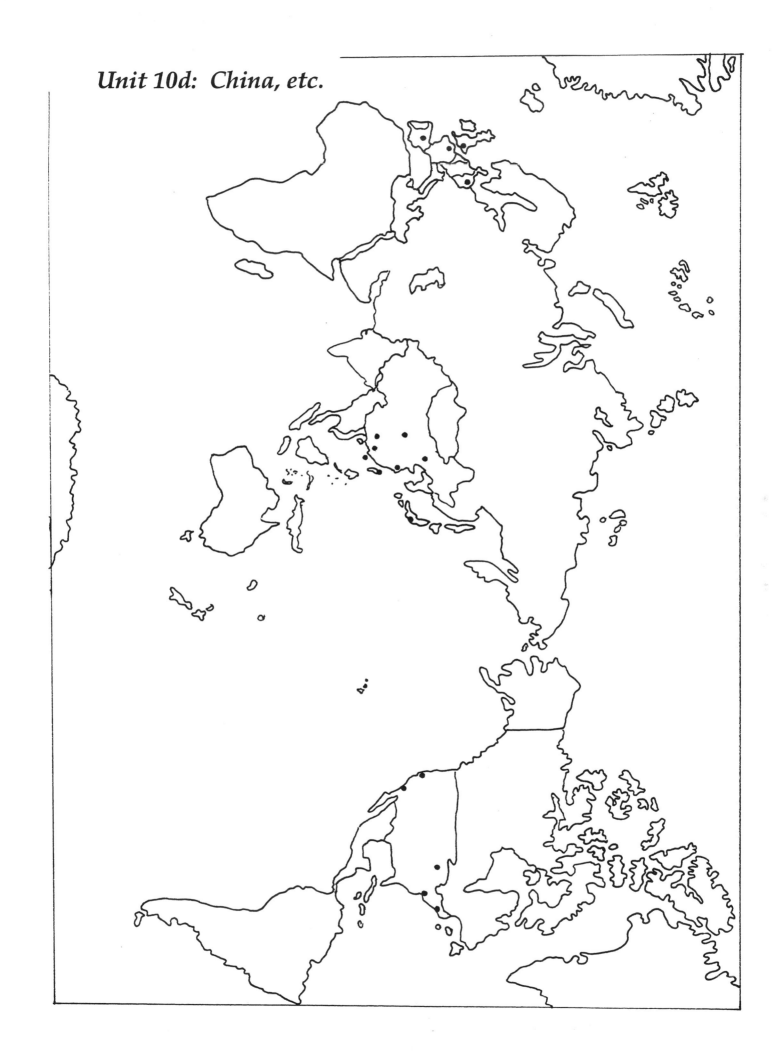

Unit 10d: China, etc.

Unit 10d: Hot & cold (A)

You have a partially completed chart of the estimated normal minimum temperatures for January for a number of cities. Your partner has a similar chart, but with somewhat different information, although there is some overlap in the information the two of you possess.

Pool your information with your partner, by asking comparative questions (<u>Běijīng bǐ Shànghái lěng ma? Běijīng bǐ Bólín nuǎnhuó ma?)</u> Your task is to rank-order the cities, from 1 to 17, with 1 being the coldest and 17 being the warmest city in winter. **YOU MAY NOT STATE ANY TEMPERATURE FIGURES.**

Rank order		Mean temperature (fahrenheit/centigrade)
_____	New York City	
_____	Chicago	14°F / -10°C
_____	San Francisco	
_____	Los Angeles	48°F / 9° C
_____	Washington, D.C.	28°F / -2°C
_____	Beijing	24°F / -5°C
_____	Xi'an	30°F / -1°C
_____	Guilin	46°F / 8°C
_____	Shanghai	
_____	Canton	55°F / 13°C
_____	Taipei	59°F / 15°C
_____	Hongkong	
_____	Tokyo	29°F / -2°C
_____	London	35°F / 2°C
_____	Paris	32°F / 0°C
_____	Berlin	26°F / -3°C
_____	Madrid	33°F / 1°C

Unit 10d: Hot & cold (B)

You have a partially completed chart of the estimated normal minimum temperatures for January for a number of cities. Your partner has a similar chart, but with somewhat different information, although there is some overlap in the information the two of you possess.

Pool your information with your partner, by asking comparative questions (<u>Běijīng bǐ Shànghái lěng ma? Běijīng bǐ Bólín nuǎnhuó ma?</u>) Your task is to rank-order the cities, from 1 to 17, with 1 being the coldest and 17 being the warmest city in winter. **YOU MAY NOT STATE ANY TEMPERATURE FIGURES.**

Rank order		Temperature
_____	New York City	26°F / -3°C
_____	Chicago	14°F / -10°C
_____	San Francisco	42°F / 6°C
_____	Los Angeles	
_____	Washington, D.C.	28°F / -2°C
_____	Beijing	
_____	Xi'an	30°F / -1°C
_____	Guilin	46°F / 8°C
_____	Shanghai	32°F / 0°C
_____	Canton	55°F / 13°C
_____	Taipei	59°F / 15°C
_____	Hongkong	56°F / 13°C
_____	Tokyo	
_____	London	35°F / 2°C
_____	Paris	32°F / 0°C
_____	Berlin	26°F / -3°C
_____	Madrid	

Unit 10d: Hot & cold (Key)

Rank order		Mean temperature (fahrenheit/centigrade)
_____	New York City	26°F / -3°C
_____	Chicago	14°F / -10°C
_____	San Francisco	42°F / 6°C
_____	Los Angeles	48°F / 9° C
_____	Washington, D.C.	28°F / -2°C
_____	Beijing	24°F / -5°C
_____	Xi'an	30°F / -1°C
_____	Guilin	46°F / 8°C
_____	Shanghai	32°F / 0°C
_____	Canton	55°F / 13°C
_____	Taipei	59°F / 15°C
_____	Hongkong	56°F / 13°C
_____	Tokyo	29°F / -2°C
_____	London	35°F / 2°C
_____	Paris	32°F / 0°C
_____	Berlin	26°F / -3°C
_____	Madrid	33°F / 1°C

Unit 10e

Materials required

• Reprints of the masters provided.

Introduction

• Use Pantomime.

Comprehension Drills

• Use Pantomime or Picture-card drills.

Oral Practice

• The students divide into small groups of 3-4, and play Simon Says, using the vocabulary in this lesson for commands (zoulu qu; qi motuo che qu). The student playing "Simon" may wish to use his/her picture cards for cue cards. The "tag" can be a phrase you wish the students to drill, such as "Qing ni..." or "Gen wo yikuar...," to take the place of "Simon Says."

• The students form pairs. Each partner receives a copy of "Getting there is half the fun," and together they complete the task assigned.

• Have the students listen to the audiotape and complete the Dialog Practice exercise for homework. Check in class.

• Divide the class into groups of 4 to rehearse "Farewell." Have one group perform.

• Brainstorm for variations of the sample statements and questions provided.

Controlled use

• The students form pairs. Each partner receives a copy of "Past experiences," and together they complete the task assigned. After all the interviews are over, take a tally of the class: Shei hùi kaiche? etc. Each student responds ON BEHALF OF THE PERSON S/HE INTER-VIEWED: Moumou rén hùi kaiche / Moumou rén zuòguò chuán / Shì zuò dào moumou dìfang de. You may wish to tally their responses on the board or overhead projector.

Unit 10e: Getting there is half the fun.

Pretend you and your partner are both gadabouts who like to travel to many different places by using different means of transportation. You both intend to travel to each of the places in the questions below, within the next month. Respond to the questions by writing the numbers corresponding to the modes of transportation in the blanks provided in column A. Try to select each of the modes of transportation once. Next, ask the questions of your partner, and record his/her responses in column B. Your partner will also ask the questions of you; respond in sentences (<u>Wǒ zuò chuán qù</u> or <u>Zuò chuán qù</u>), not phrases (<u>zuò chuán</u>). Check yourselves when you are done by comparing papers.

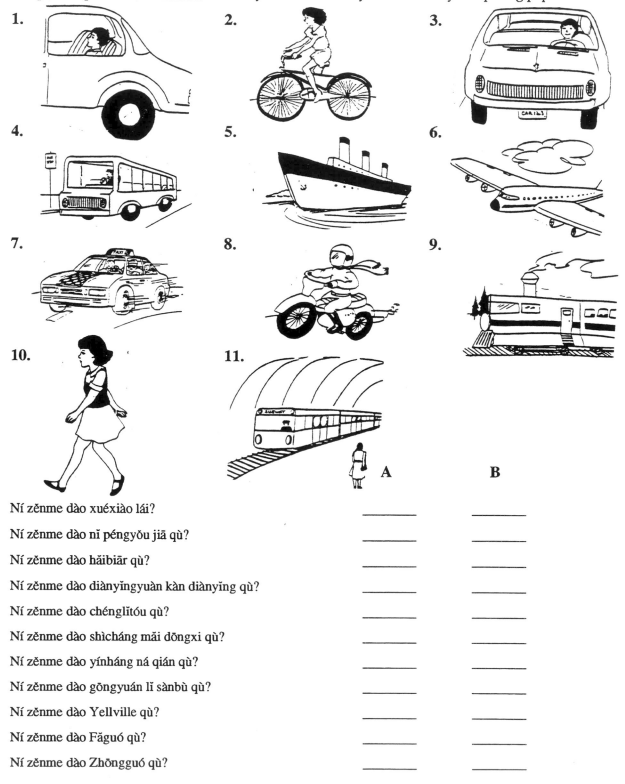

	A	B
Nǐ zěnme dào xuéxiào lái?	_____	_____
Nǐ zěnme dào nǐ péngyǒu jiā qù?	_____	_____
Nǐ zěnme dào hǎibiār qù?	_____	_____
Nǐ zěnme dào diànyǐngyuàn kàn diànyǐng qù?	_____	_____
Nǐ zěnme dào chénglǐtóu qù?	_____	_____
Nǐ zěnme dào shìcháng mǎi dōngxi qù?	_____	_____
Nǐ zěnme dào yínháng ná qián qù?	_____	_____
Nǐ zěnme dào gōngyuán lǐ sànbù qù?	_____	_____
Nǐ zěnme dào Yellville qù?	_____	_____
Nǐ zěnme dào Fǎguó qù?	_____	_____
Nǐ zěnme dào Zhōngguó qù?	_____	_____

Unit 10e: Past experiences.

Interview your partner to find out his/her past experience with modes of transportation. Record the responses either by circling an appropriate answer, or by filling in the blank. Be prepared to report on your partner's experiences in class.

	(no)	(yes)
1. Nǐ huì kāichē ma?	Búhùi kāi.	Hùi kāi.
2. Nǐ zuòguò qìchē ma? Zuòguò shéide qìchē?	Méi zùoguò.	Zuòguò.
_____ (In whose car did you ride?)		
3. Nǐ zuòguò chūzū qìchē ma? Shénme shíhòu zuòde?	Méi zùoguò.	Zuòguò.
_____ (When did you take a cab?)		
4. Nǐ zuòguò huǒche ma? Zài nǎr zuòde?	Méi zùoguò.	Zuòguò.
_____ (Where were you when you rode the train?)		
5. Nǐ zuòguò gōnggòng qìchē ma? Zài nǎr zuòde?	Méi zùoguò.	Zuòguò.
_____ (Where were you when you rode the bus?)		
6. Nǐ zuòguò dìtiě ma? Zài nǎr zuòde?	Méi zùoguò.	Zuòguò.
_____ (Where were you when you rode the subway?)		
7. Nǐ qíguò mótuōchē ma? Qíguò shéide mótuōchē?	Méi qíguò.	Qíguò.
_____ (In whose car did you ride?)		
8. Nǐ hùi qí zìxíngchē ma?	Búhùi qí.	Hùi qí.
9. Nǐ zuòguò fēijī ma? Zuò dào nǎr qù de?	Méi zùoguò.	Zuòguò.
_____ (Where were you going when you took the plane?)		

Key to dialogue puzzles

Unit 1

I.   A — B.1
II.   A — B.2 — A.1
III.   A — B.2 — A.2
IV.   A — B.1 — A.2 — B.1
V.   A — B.2 — A.1 — B.2

Unit 2a

I.   A — B.2 — A.1
II.   A — B.1 — A.1 — B.2
III.   A — B.2 — A.1 — B.2
IV.   A — B.2 — A.1 — B.1
        — A.1
V.   A — B.2 — A.1 — B.2

Unit 2b

I.   A — B.2
II.   A — B.2 — A.2
III.   A — B.1 — A.2 — B.2
IV.   A — B.2 — A.1 — B.2
V.   A — B.1 — A.2

Unit 2c

I.   A — B.2
II.   A — B.2 — A.1 — B.2
III.   A — B.1 — A.2 — B.2
IV.   A — B.1 — A.1
V.   A — B.1 — A.1 — B.2

Unit 2d

I.   A — B.2 — A.1 — B.2
II.   A — B.2 — A.1
III.   A — B.1 — A.1 — B.2
IV.   A — B.2 — A.1 — B.2
V.   A — B.1 — A.2 — B.2

Unit 2e

I.   A — B.2 — A.2 — B.1
        — A.1
II.   A — B.2 — A.1 — B.2
III.   A — B.1 — A.2 — B.1
IV.   A — B.1 — A.1 — B.1
V.   A — B.1 — A.1 — B.2

Unit 2f

I.   A — B.1 — A.2 — B.1
        — A.1
II.   A — B.2 — A.1 — B.2
III.   A — B.2 — A.1 — B.1
IV.   A — B.1 — A.1 — B.1
V.   A — B.2 — A.2 — B.1

Unit 2g

I.   A — B.2 — A.2 — B.1
        — A.2
II.   A — B.1 — A.1 — B.1
III.   A — B.2 — A.1 — B.1
IV.   A — B.1 — A.2 — B.2
V.   A — B.1 — A.2 — B.1

Unit 2h

I.   A — B.2 — A.2 — B.1
II.   A — B.1 — A.2 — B.1
III.   A — B.2 — A.2 — B.1
IV.   A — B.1 — A.1 — B.2
V.   A — B.2 — A.2 — B.1

Unit 3a

I.   A — B.2 — A.1 — B.2
II.   A — B.2 — A.1
III.   A — B.2 — A.1 — B.2
IV.   A — B.1 — A.1 — B.1
V.   A — B.2

Unit 3b

I. A — B.2 — A.2 — B.1
    — A.2
II. A — B.1 — A.2 — B.2
III. A — B.1 — A.1 — B.2
IV. A — B.2 — A.2 — B.2
    — A.2
V. A — B.2

Unit 4a

I.   A — B.1 — A.2 — B.1
     — A.2 — B.2
II. A — B.1 — A.2 — B.1
III. A — B.2 — A.1 — B.2
IV. A — B.1 — A.2 — B.2
V.   A — B.2 — A.2

Unit 4b

I.   A — B.2 — A.2 — B.1
     — A.1 — B.2
II. A — B.2 — A.1 — B.2
III. A — B.2 — A.1 — B.1
IV. A — B.2 — A.1 — B.2
V.   A — B.1 — A.1 — B.2

Unit 4c

I.   A — B.2 — A.1 — B.2
II. A — B.2 — A.2 — B.1
III. A — B.2 — A.2 — B.1
IV. A — B.1 — A.2 — B.1
V.   A — B.1 — A.2 — B.1

Unit 4d

I.   A — B.1 — A.1 — B.1
     — A.2 — B.2
II. A — B.1 — A.2 — B.2
III. A — B.2 — A.1 — B.1
IV. A — B.1 — A.2 — B.1
V.   A — B.1 — A.1 — B.2

Unit 4e

I.   A — B.2 — A.1 — B.1
     — A.1 — B.2
II. A — B.1 — A.2 — B.1
III. A — B.2 — A.1 — B.2
IV. A — B.2 — A.1 — B.2
V.   A — B.1 — A.2 — B.1

Unit 5a

I.   A — B.2 — A.2 — B.1
     — A.1
II. A — B.1 — A.2 — B.1
III. A — B.2
IV. A — B.2 — A.1 — B.2
V.   A — B.1 — A.1 — B.2

Unit 5b

I.   A — B.1 — A.1 — B.1
     — A.2 — B.2
II. A — B.2 — A.2 — B.1
III. A — B.2 — A.2 — B.1
IV. A — B.1 — A.2 — B.1
V.   A — B.1 — A.1 — B.2

Unit 5c

I.   A — B.1 — A.2 — B.2
     — A.1 — B.2
II. A — B.1 — A.1 — B.2
III. A — B.2 — A.2 — B.1
IV. A — B.1 — A.1 — B.2
V.   A — B.1 — A.1 — B.2

Unit 5d

I.   A — B.2 — A.1 — B.1
II. A — B.2 — A.1 — B.2
     — A.1 — B.2
III. A — B.2 — A.2 — B.1
IV. A — B.1 — A.1 — B.1
V.   A — B.1 — A.2 — B.1

Unit 5e

I.   A — B.2 — A.2 — B.1
     — A.2 — B.2
II. A — B.1 — A.2 — B.1
III. A — B.1 — A.2 — B.1
IV. A — B.1 — A.1 — B.1
V.   A — B.2 — A.1 — B.1

Unit 6a

I.   A — B.1 — A.2 — B.1
     — A.2
II. A — B.2 — A.1 — B.2
III. A — B.2 — A.2 — B.1
IV. A — B.1 — A.2 — B.2
V.   A — B.1

Unit 6b

I.   A — B.1 — A.1 — B.2
II. A — B.2 — A.2 — B.1
III. A — B.1 — A.1 — B.1
     — A.1
IV. A — B.1 — A.2
V.   A — B.2 — A.2 — B.1

Unit 7a

I.   A — B.2 — A.2 — B.1
II. A — B.2 — A.1 — B.1
     — A.2 — B.2
III. A — B.1 — A.1 — B.1
IV. A — B.1 — A.1 — B.2
V.   A — B.2 — A.1 — B.2
     — A.2 — B.2

Unit 7b

I.   A — B.1 — A.2 — B.1
     — A.1 — B.2
II. A — B.1 — A.2 — B.1
III. A — B.2 — A.2 — B.1
IV. A — B.2 — A.1 — B.2
V.   A — B.2 — A.1 — B.1

Unit 7c

I.   A — B.2 — A.1 — B.1
II. A — B.2 — A.1 — B.1
III. A — B.1 — A.1 — B.2
IV. A — B.2 — A.1 — B.1
     — A.2 — B.2
V.   A — B.1

Unit 7d

I.   A — B.2 — A.1 — B.2
II. A — B.1 — A.1 — B.1
III. A — B.1 — A.1 — B.2
     — A.2 — B.2
IV. A — B.2 — A.2 — B.2
V.   A — B.1

Unit 8a

I.   A — B.2 — A.2 — B.1
     — A.1 — B.1
II. A — B.1 — A.2 — B.2
III. A — B.2 — A.2 — B.2
IV. A — B.2
V.   A — B.1 — A.2 — B.2

Unit 8b

I.   A — B.2 — A.1 — B.2
     — A.1 — B.1
II. A — B.2 — A.2 — B.1
III. A — B.1 — A.2 — B.1
IV. A — B.2 — A.1 — B.2
V.   A — B.1 — A.2 — B.2

Unit 8c

I.   A — B.1 — A.2 — B.1
II. A — B.2 — A.1 — B.1
III. A — B.1 — A.2 — B.2
IV. A — B.1 — A.2 — B.1
V.   A — B.2 — A.1 — B.2

Unit 8d

I.   A — B.2 — A.2 — B.1
II. A — B.1 — A.1 — B.2
III. A — B.2 — A.2 — B.1
IV. A — B.2 — A.2 — B.1
V.   A — B.1 — A.1 — B.2

Unit 9a

I.   A — B.2 — A.2 — B.2
II. A — B.1 — A.2 — B.1
III. A — B.1 — A.1 — B.2
IV. A — B.2 — A.1 — B.2
     — A.2 — B.2
V.   A — B.1 — A.1 — B.2

Unit 9b

I.   A — B.2 — A.2 — B.1
     — A.1 — B.1
II. A — B.1 — A.1 — B.2
III. A — B.1 — A.2 — B.2
IV. A — B.2 — A.1 — B.1
V.   A — B.2 — A.2 — B.1

Unit 9c

I.   A — B.2 — A.1 — B.1
II. A — B.2 — A.2 — B.2
III. A — B.1 — A.2 — B.1
IV. A — B.1 — A.1 — B.2
V.   A — B.2 — A.1 — B.2
     — A.1 — B.1

Unit 9d

I.   A — B.1 — A.1 — B.2
II. A — B.2 — A.2 — B.1
III. A — B.2 — A.1 — B.1
IV. A — B.2 — A.2 — B.2
V.   A — B.2 — A.1 — B.2

Unit 10a

I.   A — B.2 — A.2 — B.2
     — A.1 — B.2
II. A — B.1 — A.1 — B.1
III. A — B.2 — A.1 — B.2
IV. A — B.1 — A.2 — B.2
V.   A — B.2 — A.1 — B.2

Unit 10b

I.   A — B.2 — A.2 — B.2
II. A — B.2 — A.1 — B.1
III. A — B.1 — A.2 — B.1
IV. A — B.2 — A.1 — B.1
V.   A — B.1 — A.1 — B.2

Unit 10c

I.   A — B.2 — A.1 — B.2
     — A.2 — B.2
II. A — B.2 — A.1 — B.1
III. A — B.1
IV. A — B.2
V.   A — B.1 — A.2 — B.1

Unit 10d

I.   A — B.2 — A.2 — B.1
II. A — B.1 — A.1 — B.1
III. A — B.2 — A.2 — B.1
IV. A — B.1 — A.2 — B.1
     — A.1 — B.2
V.   A — B.2 — A.1 — B.1

Unit 10e

I.   A — B.1 — A.2 — B.2
     — A.1 — B.2
II. A — B.2 — A.2 — B.1
III. A — B.1 — A.2 — B.1
IV. A — B.1 — A.1 — B.1
V.   A — B.2 — A.2 — B.2

APPENDIX: Sample Role-plays

(have your students practice carrying out these tasks near the end of the year,
or as appropriate during the year)

You have spent some time on an outdoor activity with some people
you haven't met before, but whom you like quite well. During a
break, one of them asks you about yourself. State your name, and
tell as much as you can about your personal background: where
you come from, what you do, your family, etc.

_____

You are spending a few days with the relatives of some friends, in
a city you have not been to before. They would like to know your
interests and hobbies, so that they can help plan your stay. Describe what you like to do in your spare time.

_____

You run into an elderly woman, who turns out to be a friend of
your mother's from her childhood. Describe everyone in your
family to her, and say something about what each one is doing.

_____

You are taking your classmate along to see a movie with your best
friend. At the last moment, something comes up, and you will
have to be late to the movie. Your classmate and friend have never
met before, but will have to go ahead without you, and save you a
seat. Describe your best friend's physical appearance to your
classmate.

_____

You have a visitor from a foreign country. Describe to this visitor
what it is you do, on a typical work or school day, from the time
you get up in the morning to the time you go to bed at night.

You are talking to a foreign visitor, who is considering coming to your school as an exchange student. Describe to this visitor your typical academic calendar. Include dates when semesters begin and end, time and duration of holidays, and information about key dates during the year.

You have agreed to tutor someone for a total of twenty hours during the next four weeks. Describe your plans for the next four weeks, so that you and your tutee can decide when the two of you should meet.

You have spilled a mug of hot chocolate on yourself, and have ruined what you are wearing. It is your favorite outfit. Your rich and generous aunt happens to be on her way to do some shopping. Call her, and describe to her exactly what you are wearing, so that she can replace the items for you. Include information about color, pattern, size, and anything else that would help.

You have been asked to cook an egg dish for four friends this evening. You have access to a kitchen and utensils, but no food. Tell one of your friends exactly what to buy at the supermarket, to allow you to prepare your dish.

You have invited your classmates to a party at your house. Give them directions to drive from the building in which your classroom is located to your house.

You have made an appointment with a foreign exchange student to have lunch at the student center cafeteria. Give the student directions to walk from your classroom building to the cafeteria.

- -

Your family has made arrangements to exchange your home this summer with a family in another city. You are on the telephone to this other family. Describe your house, including information on the number and types of rooms, the layout, and the general location of the house.

- -

You have made arrangements to let a foreign exchange student have your room for a semester. You are on the telephone to this student. Describe your room, including information on size, layout, and furnishings available.

- -

You are helping a high school foreign exchange student decide whether to attend the high school you attended. Describe the curriculum (as you remember it) of your last year in high school.

- -

Order a meal in a Chinese restaurant for 10 people.